Spiritual Warfare

SISTER EMMANUEL

Spiritual Warfare

The Express Lane to Union With God

children
of
Medjugorje

Translated from French by *Alexandra Schmidt*
Edited by *Ann-Marie Chinnery*
Cover design by *Nancy Cleland*
Book design by *Catholic Way Publishing*

Ordering Information:
Orders by trade bookstores and wholesalers.
Please contact Ingram Content at www.ingramcontent.com.

ISBN-13: 978-1-7363308-0-7 (PAPERBACK)
ISBN-13: 978-1-7363308-1-4 (KINDLE E-BOOK)
ISBN-13: 978-1-7363308-2-1 (EPUB E-BOOK)

10 9 8 7 6 5 4 3 2 1

Available in E-Book.

www.childrenofmedjugorje.com
USA: 2400 E. Main Street, 103-156,
St. Charles, IL 60174, USA

Thank you for your little pamphlet on spiritual warfare. It seems to me to be very educational, and the quotes from the Saints and the Desert Fathers are quite relevant It is clear that, more than ever, now is the time for spiritual warfare I am very pleased to give you a *Nihil Obstat*.

MGR. MARC AILLET, BISHOP OF BAYONNE, FRANCE, 9 MAY 2020

Contents

Introduction

"Put on the whole armor of God that you may be able to stand against the wiles of the devil. For we are not contending against flesh and blood, but against the principalities, against the powers, against the world rulers of this present darkness, against the spiritual hosts of wickedness in the heavenly places." (EPH 6:11)

St. Paul's exhortation in his Letter to the Ephesians clearly sets the tone; from the outset, we are warned and cautioned: the Christian life, where prayer is the cutting edge, draws us onto a battlefield and calls us to fight an actual battle. The adversary, the Devil, is named and exposed. We learn that he is a sneaky, powerful and invisible angel. We then find ourselves a bit like little David against Goliath. But we are not alone in this struggle: God himself protects us with the armor of his love, and we receive weapons from him that enable us to resist and be victorious.

One of the first things we must be aware of is that this battle is first and foremost a struggle against ourselves, against the passions that arouse us, the wounds that have harmed us, the negative consequences and tendencies they may have generated within us (doubt, sadness, anger, jealousy, revolt, violence, despair, etc.).. These are the precise points where the fight will take place. Each one of us is unique, but the pattern is always the same for everyone. It is the pattern which, in Christ, leads us to a profound reconciliation with ourselves, and ultimately to that peace surpassing all understanding (PHIL 4:7) that only God can give us. But this peace will only be granted in a deep and lasting way after a long and often difficult struggle.

Why is this so? Why is so much at stake in prayer that you may even be called to "resist to the point of shedding your blood" (HEB 12:4)?

1. Prayer is union with God, it is absolutely vital

We know that prayer is THE perfect way of achieving union with God, which is what every human soul is called to do, as it was created for an eternity of love with its God and Creator. God created man to fulfill his blessings and live in perfect communion with him. So the stakes are high. Our happiness depends on this. Deep down we know it, because this thirst for fullness, this thirst for true love is etched within every one of us like the seal of the Creator. Whether we are believers or not, prayer is always on our heels. Prayer is the place where union can be experienced, and where the torrents of divine tenderness can pour into our hearts.

Is it that simple? Unfortunately not, because there are many obstacles! The most common are external; the most subtle are within us.

2. Satan tries to oppose prayer with all his might

St. Peter expresses it well in a real-life metaphor: "Discipline yourselves, keep alert. Like a roaring lion your adversary the devil prowls around, looking for someone to devour". (1 PETER 5:8)

First of all, Satan will often tell us that there are better things to do than to pray, tangible things for which we will see results or immediate effectiveness. For instance, you might be seized by an irresistible hunger or thirst, or suddenly fall asleep, have to make a phone call or send an email that has suddenly become indispensable and urgent, you may be tempted to go and visit a suffering brother . . . You will easily recognize the signature of the Evil One, because these kinds of thoughts only occur at the precise moment when we are heading to church. Delays, diversions . . . anything that will make us lose sight of the absolute urgency of prayer.

Once these first obstacles are unmasked and overcome, Satan will change his tactic, and attack more sneakily from within.

Once we are settled, kneeling and collected, he may, for instance, let us recite beautiful sentences routinely, without putting our hearts into them. He also likes to inspire us with a great plan, a perfect menu for the next day, an important purchase or an ideal way to solve a current problem! Sometimes we even think that such thoughts are divine inspirations, not realizing that they simply prevent a dialogue with God.

The Evil One can also suggest to our conscience that our prayer is null and void, tormenting us with the throbbing memory of already confessed sins that alter our dialogue with the Lord by locking us in a diabolical guilt trip that cuts us off from God's love.

Another classic process is imaginary conversations: we get caught up in endless discussions with some person or other who makes us angry, who is causing us to suffer an injustice, or even with people we love and with whom we project ourselves into an illusory situation. These are all parasitical thoughts that, once again, drag us out of the present moment, the very moment when God is there and gives himself.

The Evil One excels at inspiring us with impure thoughts, so we are tempted to stop and indulge in them. He also likes to place magnifying glasses on our noses that distort situations and disconnect us from reality; everything then becomes a drama, we lose peace, and with it the presence of God. And then there is catastrophizing anxiety, which makes us imagine difficulties, suffering, even a great misfortune, events that will never occur, but which will disturb our mind and inflict unnecessary suffering and anguish. Again, all of this will take us further away from God.

Using our wounded psychology, Satan can obsess us and force our mind to stop at recurrent thoughts or unwanted images, which we find impossible to chase away or dominate. God can allow this in the night of the mind; we then need to patiently wait for the hour of liberation, an hour that God alone determines, for our sake. At that moment, the soul does not know that God is with it, but he is more present to the soul than ever. A fine example is given in the life of Catherine of Siena. Locked up by her family in a dungeon, she suffered terrible attacks from Satan. For three days and three nights, he forced upon her the vision of very impure scenes that she could not chase away despite her valiant efforts. In vain did she call for God's help. The feeling she had then of God's absence made her suffer greatly. At the end of this ordeal, she asked Jesus where he was during those three days. "I was in your heart," he replied. Jesus then enabled her to understand that the reason she had been able to avoid the sin of indulging in these impure visions, that she had been able to win against Satan, was thanks to his presence within her, even though hidden.

Satan also uses false light: disguised as an angel of light, he may inspire us with thoughts, words or actions, or revelations that will flatter our ego, exalt our self and subtly inflate us with pride. This is a crucial indicator to recognize the actions of the Evil one. True visions and real apparitions do not provide this kind of pleasure in the moment. On the contrary, they generate fear. All the prophets in the Bible clearly show this.

Conversely, the other facet of this temptation will submerge us in desolation and lock us into a false and negative image of ourselves: we are worthless, we will never achieve anything, how could God love us, what is the point of praying? It begins with discouragement and can lead to despair. These are signs that the Evil One is at work.

During prayer, Satan may also try to infect our old or current wounds, or try to sow the poisons with which he is himself filled, and make us experience sadness, bitterness, despair, revolt, doubting God's love, jealousy, etc. As always, you recognize a tree by its fruits. The good Spirit will inspire us to offer our wounds and contemplate those of Jesus instead.

Of course the enemy has an unlimited supply of tricks that are perfectly suited to our personality, to our mindset and our type of activity.

3. Weapons for victory

"Therefore, take up the whole armor of God, so that when the day of evil comes you may be able to stand your ground, and having done everything, to stand firm. Stand therefore, and fasten the belt of truth around your waist, and put on the breastplate of righteousness. As shoes for your feet put on whatever will make you ready to proclaim the gospel of peace. With all of these, take the shield of faith, with which you will be able to quench all the flaming arrows of the Evil One. Take the helmet of salvation, and the sword of the Spirit, which is the word of God." (EPH 6:13-17)

As concerns the spiritual struggle in prayer, our perfect model, the model we are called to follow, is of course Jesus Christ Himself. He experienced all things as do we, except sin. The Letter to the Hebrews gives us this assurance: "For because he himself has suffered when tempted, he is able to help those who are being tempted". (HEBREWS 2:18)

DURING THE TEMPTATION IN THE DESERT, the Devil himself tried everything to deflect Jesus from His mission. He was hungry, so that is what the first temptation focused on.

Here Satan used all the needs and attractions that we have as human beings, such as food and other bodily needs. He urged Christ to seek and revel in magical powers, a deviation from the mission of salvation for which He was sent. This refers us, for instance, to preferring the magic of Satan, even if we don't call it by that name, when God seems not to answer us in prayer.

THE SECOND TEMPTATION is about omnipotence: "If you are the Son of God, throw yourself down" (from the pinnacle of the temple.) Jesus did not want to sink into the illusory exaltation of the self. He said: "For all who exalt themselves will be humbled, and those who humble themselves will be exalted" (LUKE 14:11) and invites us, in prayer, not to fall into the trap of thoughts that flatter our pride.

Satan's ultimate goal is to take God's place and be worshipped. This is what the LAST TEMPTATION OF JESUS teaches us. This is what we are called to resist, sometimes in a subtle way when, for example, being appointed to a position of responsibility, receiving some power, a gift or a charisma becomes an end in itself that is disconnected from serving God and neighbor. Simon the Magician's request is a perfect example (ACTS 8:19). Even asking for a spiritual good like the outpouring of the Holy Spirit for nothing but personal enjoyment detracts us from God's will, playing into the hands of the enemy.

THE AGONY AT GETHSEMANE teaches us first of all that we are invited to "Watch and pray so as not to fall into temptation" – which clearly shows that it is in the very depths of prayer that we can draw the strength to resist the tactics of the devil.

And it also shows how God himself then comes to our aid. This crucial moment in Jesus' life gives us leave to rely on him in prayer to get through the anguish and trauma from the most dreadful events. We can then continue to trust the Father and persevere in prayer, despite Satan who wants to prove to us that all is lost.

FROM HIS ULTIMATE TEMPTATION, ON MOUNT GOLGOTHA, we learn that the adversary wants us to doubt the love of God, his existence and the existence of Heaven. What he wants is to lock us into abysmal despair and make our baptismal life meaningless. The Evil One thus seeks to prevent us from giving our lives in full, by suggesting that it makes no sense and serves no purpose ("Come down from the cross if you are the Son of God!").

Jesus gives us the key to victory: total surrender of the self into the hands of the Father.

The WORD OF GOD IS ONE OF THE MAJOR WEAPONS IN THIS STRUGGLE, it was used by Jesus Christ during the temptation in the desert. Relying on the Word of God is incredibly powerful when facing temptations! This is called the antirrhetic method. It consists in quoting a passage from Scripture in response to a temptation that presents itself to us. This is the method used by Jesus Himself, who remains in this instance our most perfect model. Satan hates this above all else, because the Word of God is truth and light. This light burns him and sends him running. The Word of God puts us back in God, establishes us in God and restores us to the truth. It is indeed this double-edged sword of which St. Paul speaks, which makes it possible to discern the intentions of the heart.

THE NAME OF JESUS is a powerful weapon to help us be victorious. Satan cannot bear the name of Jesus being invoked, because it makes Jesus (meaning "God saves") present, and it is then Jesus himself who is fighting with us. However, this is no magic trick, because we really have to attach ourselves to the Savior with all our being, and not just pay lip service to His name.

In many monasteries, both Catholic and Orthodox, the "Jesus Prayer" is recited throughout the day: "Lord, Jesus Christ, Son of God, have mercy on me, a sinner" (para 2667 Catechism of the Catholic Church). This prayer drives away the enemy, and for many people, has been a path of spiritual growth, inner healing and holiness.

THE SIGN OF THE CROSS is also highly effective. It reminds the Evil One of the place where he was definitively defeated, points him to his defeat and ultimately to his complete impotence. The sign of the cross establishes us in the circulation of Trinitarian love and restores communion with God. Here again, it is not magic, it is a movement of the heart.

PRAYING IN TONGUES can be an extremely effective weapon. When "that very Spirit intercedes with sighs too deep for words" (ROMANS 8:26), that is, when we pray in tongues, there is no more space within us for Satan. All the space is occupied by God, there is no more looking inward, no thinking, therefore no temptation. This is unshackled prayer *par excellence*. The evil one then has no hold on us. "The one who speaks in tongues does not speak to people, but to God." (ICOR 14:2)

FASTING is a key weapon against Satan. Whoever fasts frees up more space for the Holy Spirit, and thereby safeguards his prayer from interference from the enemy. That is why the Evil One does everything he can to turn us away from fasting (and is quite successful at it!) Before beginning His mission, Jesus fasted for 40 days and 40 nights. And He repeatedly recalled that, in the fight against evil spirits, fasting was key to achieving victory. Fasting clarifies and purifies our thoughts in prayer. (See the author's book entitled *'The Forgotten Power of Fasting'*).

FAITH, as a theological virtue, surrounds us with such light that Satan cannot reach us. This light of Faith is a veritable shield, as St. Paul reminds us in the letter to the Ephesians: " . . . take the shield of faith, with which you will be able to quench all the flaming arrows of the Evil One." (EPH 6:14). In the depths of her dark night of the soul, valiant little Thérèse of Lisieux, even though Satan suggested to her that Heaven did not exist and that she would sink ever deeper into darkness, said, "I believe what I want to believe."

THE ROSARY is considered by many saints to be a very powerful weapon against the enemy. This contemplation of Christ in the different moments of His life shifts us away from ourselves and directs our soul to the Lord. The Evil One no longer has any space to do his dirty work, he loses the leeway he needs to harm us since the soul is occupied by Christ, i.e. by the One who defeated him forever. We know that we become what we contemplate! In Medjugorje, Mary entrusted this beautiful insight to the seers: "When I was on earth, I prayed the Rosary constantly." In answer to the question "How did you

do that", she replied: "I kept the eyes of my heart constantly fixed on the life of Jesus, my Son, and this is the prayer of the Rosary." A meditation that certainly enabled her to grow inwardly and to go from victory to victory!
(See Annex 1, a few messages from Mary in Medjugorje)

PADRE PIO prayed the Rosary constantly. One evening, addressing the brother who was helping him go to bed, he asked, "Brother, before you leave, get me the weapon that is in my habit." The young brother, surprised, looked to see whether there actually was a weapon in Padre Pio's clothes-pockets. The Father insisted: "Look for it, it's there!" So as not to upset him, the brother put his hand back in his pocket and said, "Father, I can find no weapon here, there is only a rosary" and the future Saint replied, "Well, is that not a weapon?"

A SINGLE GUARDIAN ANGEL is more powerful than Satan and hell combined, for the angel is in God and God is in the angel. That is why the Church so often resorts to Archangels and Angels in the spiritual struggle. They are an integral part of the exorcist's arsenal. Let us not forget the prayer of Leo XIII, called "Little Exorcism", which begins with a long invocation to St. Michael the Archangel. *(See Annex 6 for this prayer)*.

ST FAUSTINA testified: "I took a few steps, but a great number of demons blocked my path, they threatened me with terrible torments and voices were heard: 'She deprived us of everything we have worked for all these many years.' When I asked them: 'Where do you come from in such large numbers?' These evil beings answered: 'From human hearts; do not torment us.'
    Seeing their terrible hatred for me, I immediately called my

Guardian Angel for help, and instantly his clear and radiant appearance stood next to me. And he said to me, 'Do not be afraid, spouse of my Lord, without His permission these spirits will do you no harm.' Immediately the evil spirits disappeared and my faithful Guardian Angel accompanied me visibly all the way to the house. His gaze was modest and peaceful, a ray of fire gushing from his forehead." *(Diary 418-419)*

SATAN HATES SAINTS! They remind him of the many defeats they inflicted on him in order to achieve holiness. Invoking their names is extremely effective. Some exorcists have told us that the mere evocation of Maryam of Bethlehem, John Paul II or Padre Pio was enough to send the devil running. Others say that the most powerful saint is the Holy patron saint of each individual person. Many people also benefit from using relics of Saints to rout the devil.

THE VIRGIN MARY is undoubtedly the best exorcist, since she received from God himself the mission to crush the head of the serpent. Her name alone fills the Evil One with rage, not to mention her presence! Venerable Marthe Robin, a French mystic who saw the Virgin Mary at least once a week, said: "When Satan sees her coming, you should see how he collapses!" Invoking her in prayer means definitely receiving substantial support from her, for then she comes in person and prays with us. A powerful prayer, "*August Queen of Heaven*", will help us in the hardest battles, a prayer she personally inspired to a priest. (*See Annex 2*)

Because she is a mother, Our Lady is always near us, her beloved children, and she never ceases to guide us on the path of salvation, victorious over evil. To protect us from satanic attacks, she invites us to take refuge under her maternal mantle and nestle near her Immaculate Heart. As for this mantle, the Father Himself placed it on her on the day of the Annunciation, and Satan has never been able to penetrate it with his poisoned arrows. Mary is "fearsome as an army with banners" (sg 6:4) *(See Annex 3).*

THE SUPPORT OF A GOOD SPIRITUAL FATHER is necessary to fight the spiritual battle in prayer. Opening one's heart, shining a light onto the temptations that beset us, is a sure way to push back the enemy, because he hates being named and discovered. A spiritual father will help us to discern, to avoid pitfalls and to overcome difficulties. The important thing is not to be alone in the fight.

THE SACRAMENT OF RECONCILIATION cleanses us in the Blood of Christ from remnants of unforgiveness, infections with which the enemy inflames our wounds, and which poison our prayer to the point of sometimes making it impossible. It also allows us to highlight the moments when we are complicit in the temptations that beset us in prayer. As is the case, for instance, when we indulge in a thought that is alien to our prayer, instead of returning quietly to our devotion.

THE RENEWAL OF BAPTISMAL PROMISES is one of the best ways to scare away the enemy, and it is accessible to everyone. Using our free will, we take a clear stand for God and against Satan. We can and must regularly renounce the evil spirits that come to assail us, and we must do it aloud. For instance, we can use the following kinds of statements: "In the name of Jesus, I renounce the spirit of doubt, the spirit of pride, the spirit of despair, the spirit of impurity, the spirit of hatred and vengeance, the spirit of jealousy, the spirit of drowsiness" etc. *(See Annex 4 for the Baptismal Promises).*

SACRAMENTALS are all too often overlooked. Sacramentals include exorcised incense, exorcised holy water, objects that have been blessed and that we carry with us, exorcised holy salt, exorcised holy oil, etc. St. Teresa of Avila, for example, made Satan flee with holy water. We also have the example of the Miraculous Medal.

4. God only permits this warfare to the extent that it can make us grow and unite us closer to Him

All these weapons are necessary, but let us never forget that God always remains the master of everything. He is in control at all times, even when everything may sometimes seem hopeless. Jesus only faced Satan because he was sent by the Spirit to the desert, this struggle tested him and strengthened him so that he could carry out His mission. Job was tempted only with God's permission, and the fruit was immense blessings. The same is true for countless saints (Saint Anthony of the Desert, St. Benedict, St. Catherine of Siena, Little Thérèse of the Child Jesus, St. Padre Pio, venerable Marthe Robin . . .)

This is the ordinary path of the Christian life. If we look at its fruits, it always results in spiritual growth and a deeper union with God. In fact, this is the only way to become intimate with God, something he has wanted to give us from all eternity. Seen from this perspective, spiritual warfare in prayer becomes an advantage, a good that is not only necessary but indispensable. It provides us with the kind of training that eventually enables us to love God and our neighbor in truth, free from doubt, and purified. The voice of the Serpent no longer has any grip or impact on us. We then gradually become the kind of pacified and reconciled men God dreamed of when he created humanity. Saints are living examples of this, and we are all called to be like them. That is how they were victorious over Satan.

It is important, however, for this battle to be well fought!

5. The fruits of a well-fought battle

The Saints and Desert Fathers shed a great deal of light for us on spiritual warfare in prayer. They are well experienced in this matter, and it is beneficial for us to drink from this wellspring of centuries-old wisdom. (Barsanuphius, Dorotheus of Gaza, St Maryam of Bethlehem, St Benedict, St Anthony of the Desert, St Padre Pio, St Catherine of Siena, St Faustina, St. Thérèse of Lisieux, Venerable Marthe Robin, St. Teresa of Avila, St. John of the Cross, St. John Paul II . . .)

SAINT MACARIUS, an Egyptian monk of the 4th century and Desert Father, offers us a very good summary of the meaning of spiritual warfare in prayer, and the spirit in which it is to be conducted.

> "We must not take lightly what is written about Job, namely how Satan made a request about him. On his own, he could do nothing. But what does the devil say to the Lord? 'But stretch out your hand now, and touch all that he has, and he will curse you to your face.' (JOB 1:11). Job, God and the devil are still here. As soon as someone receives

God's help, is zealous and bubbling with grace, Satan asks
for him and says to the Lord, 'Because you help him and
keep him in your care, he serves you. But leave him, place
him into my hands, and we will see if he still blesses you
to your face.' Then, after the soul has been consoled, grace
withdraws, and the soul is delivered to temptations. The
devil approaches it and overwhelms it with a thousand
evils: discouragement, despair, bad thoughts (. . .). He
throws the soul into tribulation to make it cowardly and
take away hope in God. The wise soul does not despair
when it is plunged into evils and tribulations, but holds
firmly on to what it possesses, and if thousands of trials
sweep down on it, the soul endures this by saying: 'Though
he slay me, yet will I hope in him.' (JOB 13:15)

"Then, if the man perseveres to the end (. . .), the
devil has nothing to answer (. . .). Thus Satan is covered
with shame by those who endure in the tribulations and
temptations (. . .).

"Satan never ceases to fight. As long as a man lives in
this world, clothed in flesh, he is at war (. . .). The same
is true for Christians: no doubt the enemy fights them,
but they remain with Christ, they have clothed themselves
in the strength and calm from above, and do not concern
themselves with the war (. . .).

'EVEN IF THE WAR COMES OUTWARDLY, SATAN MAY
KNOCK, BUT THEY ARE SECURED WITHIN BY THE POWER
OF THE LORD' . . . Christians, even if they are tempted
outwardly, are inwardly filled with godliness and suffer
no damage. If someone has reached this degree, he has
achieved perfect charity towards Christ and the fullness
of divinity. But those who have not reached this level

still must fight internally. At times a person may rest in prayer, but at others he is in tribulation and war. The Lord wishes it that way.

"Because he is still a child, He practices him in the wars. Two things abound within him: light and darkness, rest and tribulation. He prays in rest, and a moment later he is in distress. Let the war come, it is not up to you. But it is up to you to hate evil.

"Then the Lord, seeing your mind, that you are striving, and that you love Him with your whole soul, parts death from your soul in one moment—which is not hard for Him to do—and takes you to His bosom and into the light. In a moment of time He snatches you out of the mouth of darkness, and translates you at once into His kingdom. For to God all things are easy to do in a moment of time, if only your love is set upon Him."

DOROTHEUS OF GAZA gives us this illuminating image:

"Those who must swim in the sea and know the art of swimming dive when the wave comes upon them, and let themselves go under it, until it has passed. After which they continue to swim without difficulty. If they wish to oppose the wave, it pushes them away and throws them out at a good distance. As soon as they start swimming again, a new wave comes upon them; if they still resist, there they are again, pushed and thrown back; they only get tired and don't move forward. Let them plunge under the wave, let them duck under it, and it will pass without bothering them; they will continue to swim as long as they want and accomplish what they have to do.

The same is true of temptations. When they are endured with patience and humility, they pass without harming. But if we become distressed, troubled, start accusing everyone, we make ourselves suffer by making the temptation more overwhelming for ourselves, and the result is that this temptation not only does not benefit us, but even becomes harmful."

Dorotheus of Gaza (Desert Father, sixth century in
Palestine, born in Antioch) Instructions §140

BARSANUPHIUS offers us this apothegm: To a brother who said to him: "What must I do, Father, for the struggles distress me and pressure me? "Brother, the time of war is a time of labor. Do not weaken, keep working and fighting! When the battle becomes more pressing, become more pressing yourself and cry out: 'Lord Jesus Christ, you see my helplessness and affliction, come to my aid and snatch me from those who pursue me, for I take refuge near you.' And pray to become able to serve God with a pure heart . . . "

Barsanuphius of Gaza, 6ᵗʰ century monk
revered as a saint by the Catholic Church

SAINT SILOUAN experienced very strong temptations, to the point of doubting his salvation. He received from the Lord Jesus the following explanation for his sufferings: "The proud must always suffer in this way from demons," and Jesus also gave him the means to emerge victorious from his trials: "Hold your soul in hell and do not despair"! Saint Silouan confides that this thought was of great use to him and concludes: "My mind has been purified and my soul has found rest."

(Saint Silouan, monk of Mount Athos, died in 1938)

SAINT MARYAM OF BETHLEHEM (Sister Mary of Jesus Crucified) gives the following advice to her Carmelite sisters:

> "Be very careful to keep peace in your heart, because Satan
> fishes in murky waters. My desire is for you to keep inner
> peace; ignore fears and scruples; humiliate yourself for
> what you do not do, and come to consume all the vain
> fears that I call follies in the fire of Love."
>
> "If every lamb were to see itself as the last, the Blessed
> Mother will be with it. Follow the word of Jesus. Never be
> discouraged. Satan will be furious and will come to tempt
> you: never listen to him, always listen to the Shepherd.
> Never, never listen to Satan; he is jealous. When he comes,
> humiliate yourself. If Jesus allows him to tempt you, it is
> to make you grow."

ST. FAUSTINA gave a good illustration of the word of St. Paul: "In
your struggle against sin, you have not yet resisted to the point
of shedding your blood" (HEB 12:4)" She wrote in her diary:

> "During the Holy Hour, the Lord allowed me to taste of
> his Passion. I shared the bitterness of the torment which
> filled his soul. Jesus enabled me to know how faithful the
> soul must be to prayer, in spite of torment, drought and
> temptations, because for the most part it is on this kind of
> prayer that God's plans, which are sometimes very great,
> depend. And if we do not persevere in this prayer, we
> thwart the plans that God wanted to accomplish through
> us, or within us. Let everyone remember these words: "And
> being in anguish, he prayed more earnestly" (Luke 22:44)

I always prolong a similar prayer, especially since this is in my power and in accordance with my duties." (DIARY §872)

"Despite the silence of my soul, I have fought an unceasing battle against the enemy of my soul. I constantly discover his new pitfalls, and again the fight is in full swing. In peaceful times I practice and remain watchful, so that the enemy does not surprise me defenseless; and when I see his great fury, then I remain in the fortress, that is in the Holy Heart of Jesus." (DIARY §1287)

" . . . as I was praying for sinners and offering all my sufferings, I experienced Satan's attacks. The spirit of evil could not bear that prayer. And this specter said to me, "Do not pray for sinners but for yourself, for you shall be damned." Ignoring Satan, I prayed with renewed fervor for sinners. The evil spirit shouted in anger, 'Oh, if only I had power over you!' – and he disappeared. I knew that my suffering and prayer were disturbing Satan, and I snatched many souls from his clutches." (DIARY §1465)

Jesus: "When a soul glorifies my goodness, then the demon trembles at this sight and flees to the depths of hell." (DIARY §378)

PADRE PIO also explains that the Devil cannot harm us spiritually unless we let him in: "The devil is like a rabid dog tied to a chain. Beyond the length of the chain, it can't get to anyone. You, therefore, keep your distance. If you are too close, you will be caught. Remember, the Devil has only one door to enter our soul: our will. There is no secret or hidden door. No sin is a real sin if it has not been voluntarily consented to." (*Roads to Padre Pio*)

> "Pray at all times in the Spirit, with all prayer and suppli-
> cation. To that end keep alert with all perseverance . . . "
> (EPH 6:18)

Praying constantly: this is what we are called to do, and this is what the devil opposes with all his might. This life of union in God, in abandonment and trust, can only be the result of a constant struggle that leads us to move forward from victory to victory, keeping our eyes fixed on the inexhaustible source of Love.

Annex

1. Some messages from Mary about the Rosary

When the visionary Marija Pavlovic asked her, "What is your message for priests? The Blessed Mother replied, "Dear children, I ask you to call the priests to pray the Rosary. Through the ROSARY, you will overcome all the misfortunes that Satan wants to inflict on the Catholic Church. Pray the ROSARY, all you priests. Spend time on the ROSARY" (25 JUNE 1985).

"Dear children, put on the armor for battle and with the ROSARY in your hand defeat him!" (8 AUGUST 1985).

"Pray, and let the ROSARY always be in your hand as a sign to Satan that you belong to me." (25 FEBRUARY 1988).

"Dear young people, Satan is strong and will do anything to disturb you, hindering all your initiatives. So pray more, because you need it very much in these times. The most effective weapon against Satan is the ROSARY" (1 AUGUST 1990).

"God has sent me among you so that I may help you. If you so wish, grasp for the ROSARY! Even the ROSARY alone can work miracles in the world and in your lives." (25 JANUARY 1991).

"When you are tired and sick and you do not know the meaning of your life, take the ROSARY and pray; pray until prayer becomes for you a joyful meeting with your Savior." (25 APRIL 2001).

"Pray that you can be apostles of the divine light in this time of darkness and hopelessness. This is a time of your trial. With a ROSARY in hand and love in the heart set out with me. I am leading you towards Easter in my Son." (2 MARCH 2012).

"The most beautiful thing is to see a man on his knees, with a ROSARY in his hands, because the grains of the ROSARY are a more powerful weapon than the nuclear bomb" (JELENA VASILJ'S PRAYER GROUP, 1984)

2. A Powerful Prayer

On 13 January 1864, Blessed Father Louis-Édouard Cestac (1801-1868), founder of the congregation of the Servants of Mary, was suddenly struck as if by a ray of divine clarity. He saw demons strewn across the earth, causing inexpressible havoc. At the same time, he had a vision of the Holy Virgin Mary. This good Mother told him that indeed the demons were unleashed in the world, that the time had come to pray to her as the "QUEEN OF ANGELS" and to ask her to send the heavenly legions to fight and defeat the powers of hell. He received from the Blessed Virgin the prayer "August Queen of the Heavens and Heavenly Sovereign of the Angels" which was granted indulgence by St. Pius X on 8 July 1908. (Father Cestac was beatified on 31 May 2015 in Bayonne by Cardinal Amato. His feast day is on 27 March.)

> "August Queen of Heaven, sovereign queen of Angels, you who at the beginning received from God the power and the mission to crush the head of Satan, we beseech you humbly, send your holy legions so that, on your orders and by your power, they will track down demons, fight them everywhere, curb their audacity and plunge them into the abyss. Who can be compared to God? Oh good and

tender Mother, you will always be our love and our hope. Oh divine Mother, send the Holy Angels and Archangels to defend me and to keep the cruel enemy far from me. Holy Angels and Archangels defend us, protect us. Amen."

3. Mary Comes to Help Us

"I am with you and I desire to take you into my heart and protect you, but you have not yet decided. Therefore, dear children, I am seeking for you to pray, so that through prayer you would allow me to help you . . . ." 25 January 1992

"Dear children! These days Satan is manifesting himself in a special way in this parish. Pray, dear children, that God's plan is brought into effect and that every work of Satan ends up for the glory of God. I have stayed with you this long so I might help you along in your trials." 7 February 1985

"Therefore, little children, I invite you all, to decide again today for conversion. I am close to you and I invite you all, little children, into my embrace to help you, but you do not want it and in this way, Satan is tempting you, and in the smallest things, your faith disappears. This is why little children, pray and through prayer, you will have blessing and peace." 25 March 1995

"I am close to you and I pray for each one of you and I beg you: pray, pray, pray. Only through prayer can we defeat evil and protect all that Satan wants to destroy in your lives. I am your Mother and I love you all equally, and I intercede for you before God." 25 February 1994

"Little children, comprehend that this is a time of grace for each of you; and with me, little children, you are secure. I desire to lead you all on the way of holiness. Live my messages and put into life every word that I am giving you. May they be precious to you because they come from heaven." 25 June 2002

"Dear children! Also today I call you: live your vocation in prayer. Now, as never before, Satan wants to suffocate man and his soul by his contagious wind of hatred and unrest. In many hearts there is no joy because there is no God or prayer. Hatred and war are growing from day to day. I am calling you, little children, begin anew, with enthusiasm, the walk of holiness and love; since I have come among you because of this. Together, let us be love and forgiveness . . . " 25 January 2015

"I desire, little children, for each of you to fall in love with eternal life which is your future, and for all worldly things to be a help for you to draw you closer to God the Creator. I am with you for this long because you are on the wrong path. Only with my help, little children, you will open your eyes. There are many of those who, by living my messages, comprehend that they are on the way of holiness towards eternity." 25 January 2009

"Do not forget, little children, that Satan is strong and wants to draw you away from prayer. You, do not forget that prayer is the secret key of meeting with God. That is why I am with you to lead you. Do not give up on prayer."
25 August 2017

4. Baptismal Promises

V. Do you reject Satan?
R. I do.

V. And all his works?
R. I do.

V. And all his empty promises?
R. I do.

V. Do you believe in God, the Father
Almighty, creator of heaven and earth?
R. I do.

V. Do you believe in Jesus Christ, his only Son, our
Lord, who was born of the Virgin Mary was crucified,
died, and was buried, rose from the dead, and is
now seated at the right hand of the Father?
R. I do.

V. Do you believe in the Holy Spirit, the holy Catholic Church, the communion of saints, the forgiveness of sins, the resurrection of the body, and life everlasting?
R. I do.

V. God, the all-powerful Father of our Lord Jesus Christ has given us a new birth by water and the Holy Spirit, and forgiven all our sins. May he also keep us faithful to our Lord Jesus Christ for ever and ever.
R. Amen.

5. The Popes Enlighten Us

POPE BENEDICT XVI

"This Year of Faith Lent is a favorable time for rediscovering faith in God as the basic criterion for our life and for the life of the Church. This always means a struggle, a spiritual combat, because the spirit of evil is naturally opposed to our sanctification and seeks to make us stray from God's path. For this reason the Gospel of Jesus' temptations in the wilderness is proclaimed every year on the First Sunday of Lent.

"Indeed, after receiving the "investiture" as Messiah — "Anointed" with the Holy Spirit at the baptism in the Jordan — Jesus was led into the wilderness by the Spirit himself to be tempted by the devil. At the beginning of his public ministry, Jesus had to unmask himself and reject the false images of the Messiah which the tempter was suggesting to him. Yet these temptations are also false images of man that threaten to ensnare our conscience, in the guise of suitable, effective and even good proposals. The Evangelists Matthew and Luke present three temptations of Jesus that differ slightly, but only in their order. Their

essential core is always the exploitation of God for our
own interests, giving preference to success or to material
possessions.

"The tempter is cunning. He does not directly impel
us towards evil but rather towards a false good, making
us believe that the true realities are power and everything
that satisfies our primary needs. In this way God becomes
secondary, he is reduced to a means; in short, he becomes
unreal, he no longer counts, he disappears. Ultimately, in
temptation faith is at stake because God is at stake. At the
crucial moments in life but also, as can be seen at every
moment, we stand at a crossroads: do we want to follow
our own ego or God? Our individual interests or the true
Good, to follow what is *really* good?

"As the Fathers of the Church teach us, the temptations
are part of Jesus' "descent" into our human condition,
into the abyss of sin and its consequences; a "descent"
that Jesus made to the end, even to death on the Cross
and to the hell of extreme remoteness from God. In this
way he is the hand that God stretches out to man, to the
lost sheep, to bring him back to safety. As St. Augustine
teaches, Jesus took the temptations from us to give us his
victory (cf. *Enarr. in Psalmos*, 60, 3: pl 36, 724).

"Therefore let us not be afraid either of facing the battle
against the spirit of evil: the important thing is to fight
it with him, with Christ, the Conqueror. And to be with
him let us turn to his Mother, Mary; let us call on her
with filial trust in the hour of trial and she will make us
feel the powerful presence of her divine Son, so that we

can reject temptations with Christ's word and thus put
God back at the center of our life."

(Excerpt from the Angelus of 17 February 2013)

POPE FRANCIS TELLS US

"The Christian life is a constant battle.

We are not dealing merely with a battle against the
world and a worldly mentality.

Nor can this battle be reduced to the struggle against
our human weaknesses and proclivities. It is also a constant
struggle against the devil, the prince of evil.

We will not admit the existence of the devil if we insist
on regarding life by empirical standards alone, without a
supernatural understanding.

He is present in the very first pages of the Scriptures,
which end with God's victory over the devil. God's word
invites us clearly to "stand against the wiles of the devil"
(EPH 6:11) ... These expressions are not melodramatic, precisely because our path towards holiness is a constant battle.

Along this journey, the cultivation of all that is good,
progress in the spiritual life and growth in love are the
best counterbalance to evil. For "if we start without con-
fidence, we have already lost half the battle and we bury
our talents... Christian triumph is always a cross, yet a
cross which is at the same time a victorious banner, borne
with aggressive tenderness against the assaults of evil".

(Apostolic Exhortation Gaudete et Exsultate,
November 24, 2013, n. 85)

6. Pope Leo XIII

Pope Leo XIII gives us a prayer that was composed after seeing a vision of hell

In Don Amorth's book, *An Exorcist Tells his Story*, we can read about this vision:

"On October 13, 1884, the great Pontiff Leo XIII was celebrating Holy Mass and then, as usual, attended another ceremony in thanks.

Suddenly, he was seen lifting his head and staring intensely at something above the celebrant. He stared, not batting an eye, as if filled with a sense of horror and awe, and the features of his face changed color. Something strange and huge was happening to him. Finally, as if regaining his spirits, he stood up, leaning on his hand in a light but energetic movement. We saw him heading to his private office. His anxious relatives followed him and asked him in a low voice: "Holy Father, do you not feel well? Do you need anything?" He said, "No, nothing."

Half an hour later he called the Secretary of the Congregation of Rites and handed him a sheet, ordering him to print it out and send it to all the bishops in the world. What was on that sheet? The prayer that we recite at the end of Mass

with the faithful, and which contains the Supplication to Our Lady, the burning invocation to the Prince of the Heavenly Hosts, and the imploration of God that He may cast Satan back into hell."

Here is another account from the French journal *"L'Appel du ciel"* (*The Call from Heaven*), No. 25 dated September 2010, supplemented with a few details from an almost identical account published by the journal of the Secular Order of St. Augustine in December 1941:

"On October 13, 1884, after Pope Leo XIII had finished celebrating Mass in the Vatican chapel, surrounded by a few cardinals and members of the Vatican, he suddenly stopped at the foot of the altar. He stood there for about ten minutes as if in ecstasy, his face turned white. Then, going immediately from the chapel to his office, he composed the prayer to St. Michael the Archangel with instructions that it be said after all Low Masses everywhere.

"When asked what had happened, he explained that as he was about to leave the foot of the altar, he suddenly heard voices:

"After Mass, I heard two voices, one kind and gentle, the other guttural and harsh. They seemed to be coming from near the tabernacle. *It was the devil addressing the Lord, as if in dialogue . . . Then I had a terrible vision of hell: I saw the earth as if shrouded in darkness, and from an abyss I saw a legion of demons coming out of the world to destroy the works of the Church and to attack the Church itself, which I saw on her last legs. Then St. Michael appeared and cast the evil spirits back into the abyss. After this, I saw*

St. Michael Archangel intervene not at that moment, but much later, when people had multiplied their fervent prayers to the Archangel."

At the end of this vision, Leo XIII wrote this prayer to St. Michael the Archangel, and ordered it to be recited after each Mass.

"*Saint Michael the Archangel, defend us in battle, be our protection against the wickedness and snares of the devil; may God rebuke him, we humbly pray; and do thou, O Prince of the heavenly host, by the power of God, cast into hell Satan and all the evil spirits who prowl through the world seeking the ruin of souls. Amen."*

This request was abolished in 1964, but during the Regina Caeli on Sunday, 24 April 1994, Pope John-Paul II asked the faithful to recite the prayer to St. Michael composed by Leo XIII after Mass. He spoke of the *Woman clothed in the Sun* mentioned in the Revelation of St. John, where the dragon seeks to devour her newborn son. The Pope then said, "Before woman accumulates all that threatens life . . . we must turn to the Woman clothed in the Sun and surround ourselves with her maternal care." "May prayer give us strength to face the spiritual battle mentioned in the Letter to the Ephesians: "Be strong in the Lord and in his mighty power." (EPHESIANS 6:10). And this same battle mentioned in Revelation reminds us of the image of St. Michael the Archangel. "Saint Michael the Archangel defends us in the battle against the demons and the traps they set for us."

On September 29, 2019, on the feast day of St. Michael the Archangel, Pope Francis asked all Catholics, throughout the month of the Rosary, to recite the following: a rosary, then a *Sub tuum praesidium* and the prayer to St. Michael the Archangel. Here is the prayer Sub Tuum:

> "We fly to thy patronage, O holy Mother of God; despise not our petitions in our necessities, but deliver us always from all dangers, O glorious and Blessed Virgin Mary. Amen."

Other works by the Author

These following videos are available on YouTube and on:
www.sremmanuel.org

- Devour the Book Which Tells the Truth! (27:44)

  With Sr. Emmanuel and her guest, Ralph Martin, NEW!
  (Don't miss to walk in God's Light in this time of confusion!)
  https://youtu.be/m9rQ7srO0E

- Stop, and Reflect on Your Future! (22:48) NEW!

  (An urgent appeal from Our Lady, as Eternity is at hand!)
  https://youtu.be/EmGrKCSw0Qw

- I Had an Appointment with Death at 5 pm.

  Sr. Emmanuel's Personal Testimony (37:00)
  https://www.youtube.com/watch?v=XYAub2cJWas&t=1s

- The Miracle Hidden in Your Rosary (21:12)
  https://www.youtube.com/watch?v=RCW36MwGl_c

- The Forgotten Power of Fasting (23:03)
  https://www.youtube.com/watch?v=g_FyRfrN6j4&t=243s

- Let Peace Flow to Your Heart Like a River (21:43)
  https://www.youtube.com/watch?v=4y5PCePDjgQ

- Come to Me! My Name is Mercy (34:59)
  https://www.youtube.com/watch?v=8fb-kOEcYQU

- Maïsa Arraf Sings in Arabic "Resurrection"(3:20)
  https://www.youtube.com/watch?v=-rfO8PrSvKo

- Paul, the Prayer of a Poor (13:31)
  https://www.youtube.com/watch?v=ffd0lVpzlEY

- Three Days to Defeat Death (37:54)
  https://www.youtube.com/watch?v=06gvD9k6wcU&t=264s

- Don't Miss Your Second Chance! Fr Daniele Natale (20:47)
  https://www.youtube.com/watch?v=aTxd-91pFpg

- The 24 Hours of the Gospa (12:150)
  https://www.youtube.com/watch?v=3SCyYoNqzwU

- Medjugorje in Confinement (4:36)
  https://www.youtube.com/watch?v=G5IsjZuFA-Q

- Consecrate Your Death and Heal from Fear (13:18)
  https://www.youtube.com/watch?v=xW5Nwq22FZY

- Choose Your Future; Heaven, Purgatory or Hell (25:18)
  https://www.youtube.com/watch?v=blbIte7VN4Q&t=152s

- Gratitude: the Secret to Happiness (13:43)
  https://www.youtube.com/watch?v=IXnL_MA92_A

- Sister Emmanuel Prays to Saint Joseph (13:37)
  https://www.youtube.com/watch?v=gummYHHoW44

- Forgive and be Free! (9:23)
  https://www.youtube.com/watch?v=do5c00glBKA

- Prayer to Jesus in the Womb of Mary (7:00)
  https://www.youtube.com/watch?v=RxqF5zk6ryI

- Jealousy: Commentary of Nov. 25 message, 2019 (6:24)
  https://www.youtube.com/watch?v=3cxAthNA78o

- The Chaplet of Divine Mercy (8:39)
  https://www.youtube.com/watch?v=FZa5DL05T-I

- You Had an Abortion? I have Something to Share with You! (4:50)
  https://www.youtube.com/watch?v=kncHijv_KLg

- The Power of Fasting in 10 minutes (9:26)
  https://www.youtube.com/watch?v=ROF6LxlVI_s

- Help Your Priests! (5:35)
  https://www.youtube.com/watch?v=LnbZJLuN0IM

- The Miracle of Baby Jesus (5:44)
  https://www.youtube.com/watch?v=9nPJv5tMByc

- How to Deal with Suffering (1:09:53)
  https://www.youtube.com/watch?v=Gg1AT7oy8R0

Other books from the Author

- THE FORGOTTEN POWER OF FASTING
  Healing, Liberation, Joy . . .

"I READ YOUR BOOK FROM cover to cover. Your words completely captivated me and have convinced me on the importance of fasting. I knew already the benefits of fasting, but I wasn't aware of all its attributes, that you explain so well. Reading this book one discovers fasting.

As we know, Our Lady in Medjugorje continuously insists on the importance of fasting, but we avoid putting into practice something when it means we have to make a sacrifice. We struggle to convince ourselves to actually fast.

The arguments you present, and the examples that you give in this book, show very clearly the reason why Our

Lady insists so persistently on something so precious for the soul and the body, for the apostolate on earth and for the souls in Purgatory. I thank you for emphasizing such an important topic, very often mentioned in Sacred Scripture, so precious for the living and for the intercession of the dead.

The final part of your work, with the words from the saints, will convince even the most reluctant.

This book will be nothing less than a true discovery of fasting to whoever reads it."

Don Gabriele Amorth

Euro 7.00
Sister Emmanuel
© 1995 Children of Medjugorje
www.sremmanuel.org

• CHILDREN, HELP MY
HEART TO TRIUMPH!

AT THE HEIGHT OF THE BOS-nian War, Sister Emmanuel remained in Medjugorje with a few members of her community. During that time, memories of her father, a Prisoner of War during WWII, continually surfaced. Remembering how much he suffered, she felt a need to do something to spiritually help those on the front lines. Sister Emmanuel describes a call that she received at that time to appeal to the children for their sacrifices in order to alleviate the war. *Children, Help My*

Heart To Triumph was written in response to that call. It describes for children how to make a 9-day novena of little sacrifices. Included is a coloring book that they can color and mail to Medjugorje where they will be presented at one of Our Lady's apparitions.

US $ 11.99

Sister Emmanuel

© 1996 Children of Medjugorje

Reprinted 2012 Includes Coloring Book

www.sremmanuel.org

● THE AMAZING SECRET OF THE SOULS IN PURGATORY

IT IS NOT OFTEN THAT A BOOK touches the soul so deeply. *The Amazing Secret of the Souls in Purgatory* is such a book. Maria Simma, deceased in March of 2003, lived a humble life in the mountains of Austria. When she was twenty-five, Maria was graced with a very special charism—the charism of being visited by the many souls in Purgatory—and being able to communicate with them! Maria shares, in her own words, some amazing secrets about the souls in Purgatory.

She answers questions such as: What is Purgatory? How do souls get there? Who decides if a soul goes to Purgatory? How can we help get souls released from Purgatory?

US $ 8.99
© 1997 Queenship Publishing
www.queenship.org
www.sremmanuel.org

- THE HIDDEN CHILD
  OF MEDJUGORJE

"READING "MEDJUGORJE, THE 90s" had left me dazzled and so deeply touched that it had literally pulled me to Medjugorje. I just had to see with my own eyes the spiritual wonders retold in that book. Now with "The Hidden Child," the ember of love for Mary has received a new breath of air—a Pentecostal wind. Sr. Emmanuel is indeed one of Mary's best voices! Congratulations for this jewel of a testimonial! I wouldn't be surprised if the Gospa herself turned out to be Sister's most avid reader."

Msgr. Denis Croteau, OMI

"BOOKS ARE LIKE SEASHELLS; AT first they all look alike. However, they are far from being identical and their value varies greatly. Some of them are packed with riches and so well written, that they hide rare pearls within. Sister Emmanuel's book is one of those; it contains the most beautiful pearls, and with them enriches the reader. Through her accounts and anecdotes, the reader is pleased to meet people of great worth and to be filled with the teachings of so many events. Through this book, one will explore more fully a way still too little known: the way of the Queen of Peace."

Fr. Jozo Zovko, OFM

US $ 15.99
Sister Emmanuel
© 2010 Children of Medjugorje, Inc.
www.sremmanuel.org

- MARYAM OF BETHLEHEM, THE LITTLE ARAB

WHO IS THIS LITTLE ARAB? Maryam Baouardy is a daughter of Galilee. Her life? A succession of supernatural manifestations worthy of Catherine of Sienna. Maryam shares the keys of holiness, including ways to defeat Satan himself. This is a book you don't want to miss?

US $ 5.00
Sister Emmanuel
© 2012 Children of Medjugorje, Inc.
www.sremmanuel.org
Available in E-Book

- **THE BEAUTIFUL STORY OF MEDJUGORJE**
  As Told to Children
  from 7 to 97

IN THIS BOOK, YOU WILL FOLlow the experiences of six little shepherds, their shock when they saw the "Lady" appearing to them in 1981. You will see how Vicka and Jokov actually experienced the reality of life beyond this world, when Our Lady took them with her on the most extraordinary journey to Heaven, Purgatory and Hell.

You will learn how brave they were under persecution. You will be excited to know the mes—sages they share from a

Mother who thinks only of helping us, who loves each one of us so much—including you in a very special way!

You will read about the powerful healings of bodies and souls happening there, as in Lourdes.

This is an adventure story, except that this story is true and is happening right now for you!

US $5.00

Sister Emmanuel

© 2012 Children of Medjugorje

www.sremmanuel.org

Available in E-Book

- PEACE WILL HAVE
  THE LAST WORD

THE MERCY OF GOD IS SCANDALOUS, it even borders on the extreme! In her engaging and lively style, Sister Emmanuel recounts real life stories and testimonies that take the reader's heart on a journey of God's mercy, passing through the prisons of New York, and into the confessionals of the Saints!

In these pages, a mosaic of photos and parables, the reader encounters the very depths of the human heart and is transported into the midst of scenes and situations that are as captivating as they are diverse. Through them we witness that much-desired peace that comes from Above, gaining victory over emptiness, futility and fear.

Here are words that many no longer dare to speak, and yet, they have the power to help rebuild a degenerating society. This book is a shot in the arm, an injection of hope that will hasten the time when, in the hearts of all, peace will have the last word!

US $ 13.99
Sister Emmanuel
© 2015 Children of Medjugorje
www.sremmanuel.org

- SCANDALOUS MERCY
  When God Goes Beyond
  the Boundaries

WHY SCANDALOUS MERCY?

In these pages the reader will discover unexplored aspects of the Heart of God that you might think are crazy! Crazy with love! You will meet Mother Teresa, Maryam of Bethlehem, a Nazi criminal, a priest condemned to hell, a high ranking abortionist, a drug dealer from Brazil, a furious mother-in-law, a sick child . . . and in the middle of all this, the most beautiful Heart of Christ, who is calling ALL His children.

This beautiful selection of testimonies and "little flowers" picked from everyday life will capture the reader on two levels: first, the reader of this book will find his achy heart soothed and enriched by new ways to find hope in our difficult world today; second, he will be shocked to learn that these stories are true. They will make you laugh, cry, even tremble, but one thing is certain, they will all amaze you!

US $13.00

Sister Emmanuel

© 2015 Children of Medjugorje

www.sremmanuel.org

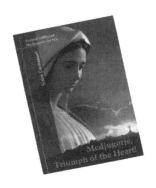

the miracles of Mary's motherly love.

US $ 12.95
Sister Emmanuel
© 2015 Children of Medjugorje
www.sremmanuel.org

- **MEDJUGORJE, TRIUMPH OF THE HEART**
  Revised Edition of
  Medjugorje of the 90s

SISTER EMMANUEL OFFERS A pure echo of Medjugorje, the eventful village where the Mother of God has been appearing since 1981. She shares at length some of the personal stories of the villagers, the visionaries, and the pilgrims who flock there by the thousands, receiving great healings. Eight years of awe have inspired this book. these 89 stories offer a glimpse into

Printed in Great Britain
by Amazon

54069631R00041

GREP in InDesign

third edition

by Peter Kahrel

A note from the Publisher:

If you know people who would benefit from this book, please refer them to *indesignsecrets.com/grepbook*. Thank you!.

3rd Edition, v2

ISBN: 978-0-9825083-8-1

Designed by Ren Reed using Adobe® InDesign.®

The typefaces used are Klinic Slab for the body text and Barlow Condensed for the chapter titles. Designed by Joe Prince, Klinic Slab is a contemporary, versatile slab-serif. Barlow Condensed is a slightly rounded, low-contrast, grotesk font superfamily designed by Jeremy Tribby.

Contents

To our readers

In this book, all GREP strings are formatted with a blue highlight in a different font, like this: `^\d+\.?\s`. Literal text strings and Find/Change results are formatted *in italics*.

Sometimes, the author adds spaces between chunks of longer GREP strings to make them easier to read, such as `(?x)  \w+  ([lst])  (ed|ing)`

In these instances you'll note that he precedes the string with `(?x)` which tells InDesign to ignore any spaces in the GREP string. He explains this in more detail in the sidebar, "Making expressions easier to read" on page 33.

Please contact us at ebooks@cpn.co to inform us of any errors, typos, or broken links that somehow escaped our close scrutiny.

Foreword

I don't know anyone who teaches GREP in InDesign who doesn't use Peter Kahrel's book – it's the "bible" on the subject! And whether you're a beginning or advanced InDesign user, this book will undoubtedly help turn you into a power user.

GREP is a set of powerful tools that let you search for text patterns, which sounds dull until you see what you can do with it! Whether you need to change the text you find (using Find/Change), or automatically apply formatting to it (using GREP Styles), these tools can dramatically speed up your work, especially with long documents.

Fortunately, while it appears complex, GREP is actually very easy to learn – especially at first. And Peter is a master at explaining the codes, offering easy-to-understand examples, and stepping you through the process of building "real world" expressions you can use immediately.

I hope you enjoy this book and get as much from it as I have. Then, when you're feeling more confident, but still have more questions, consider joining the *Treasures of GREP* group on Facebook, where you'll find a community of people who love to talk about it.

—David Blatner
co-host, InDesignSecrets.com
co-author, Real World InDesign

About This Book

This guide deals with InDesign's GREP feature, covering all InDesign versions from CS3. GREP is a stable feature; the only big change occurred in CS4 with the introduction of Unicode properties. In addition, CS4 introduced GREP styles, though these don't influence GREP expressions, only the way in which they are applied.

The first chapter, "GREP by Example", offers a quick illustration of a handful of useful features of GREP that should win you over straight away. It is followed by an outline of the organisation of the GREP dialog. We discuss here how GREP operators can be picked from lists and how Unicode characters are entered. After that, starting at the section "Wildcards", InDesign's GREP features are discussed in detail. The section "Single line and multi-line" discusses some aspects of GREP that are probably not needed very often but are nevertheless useful enough to include here. The text concludes with a section on resources, one on troubleshooting (a catalogue of my own painful experiences) and a reference section that lists all the GREP language elements.

Note: This is the re-edition of the title previously published by O'Reilly. The text is in essence the same as the O'Reilly edition. Apart from its different apprearance, the text was updated here and there to edit out references to older versions of InDesign, and the screen shots were refreshed.

— *Peter Kahrel*

1

GREP by Example

It may be easiest to see how GREP[1] works with a few examples. But first a quick comparison with InDesign's Text search, which is useful because the comparison reveals GREP's strength.

InDesign's text search is used mainly for searching literal text: when you search for *cats*, you find just that (disregarding settings such as case-sensitivity and whole-word only). But in the Text tab you can use some wildcards: ^9 finds any digit, ^$ stands for any letter, ^? matches any character, and ^w is used to find any whitespace. Thus with *Figure^w^9* you search for the literal text *Figure* followed by any space, followed by a digit. When you use any of these wildcards, you're no longer looking for literal text, but for a pattern. The four wildcards in the Text tab are useful, though rather limited – for instance, you can't use them for replacements, only for searching.

In contrast, with GREP you mainly look for patterns. For example, you can look for series of digits rather than

---

1   GREP stands for Global Regular Expression Print (or, some say "Parser"). It comes from a UNIX command-line utility that performs pattern searches in code. Most modern text editors support GREP (*aka* RegEx, for Regular Expressions) in their search and replace functions.

for a single digit. Figure \d+ matches the literal text *Figure* followed by any number (2, 34, 121, etc.): \d stands for digit, the plus sign means "at least one". The GREP expression \u\l+ finds an upper-case letter \u followed by one or more lower-case letters \l+. GREP also deals with simple alternation. For example, to find both *centre* and *center*, search for cent(re|er); alternatives are separated by pipe symbols (|). Optionality adds more flexibility: to find both the singular and plural forms of these alternatives, search for cent(re|er)s?. The question mark says that the *s* should be matched if present, otherwise not. This simple GREP, then, finds *centre*, *centres*, *center*, and *centers*.

More flexibility is offered by so-called character classes. For instance, p[aeiouy]t matches *p* followed by one vowel, followed by *t*, so you'll find *pat*, *pet*, *pit*, *pot*, and *put* (though you'll find *pyt* in *python* and *pat* in *spat* as well; we'll see later how to do whole-word-only searches). This example also demonstrates how you can define your own wildcards: here we defined a wildcard "vowel" by enclosing all vowels in brackets: [aeiouy]. Other home-made wildcards could be "ascender letter" [bdfhkl] and "descender letter" [gjpqy].

GREP expressions can be used to style text patterns. For instance, to apply a character style "smallcaps" to any sequence of two or more capitals, enter \u\u+ in the Find What field, leave the Change To field empty, and specify the style in the Change Format field. Again, \u is the wildcard for upper-case letters, and the plus stands for "one or more", so \u\u+ matches strings of at least two capital letters.

To demonstrate replacement with wildcards, let's return to the *Figure* example. To replace the word *Figure* with *Map* when it is used to refer to an illustration – that is, when it is followed by a digit – search for **Figure (\d)** and replace with **Map $1**. **\d** matches any digit, and the parentheses surrounding **\d** indicate that the contents of the parenthetical should be captured. The string **$1** in the replacement string corresponds with what was captured in the search string, so that *Figure 1* is replaced with *Map 1*, *Figure 2* with *Map 2*, etc.

As a last example, and to show that simple expressions can achieve a great deal, we'll take this seemingly difficult task: you have an address list that contains, among other things, an email address for each person. Your task is to add the word *Email:* before each email address. Let us assume for the moment that @ is used for nothing else, so that any line that contains the @ symbol is an email address.

What we need now is two expressions that combine to say "If a line contains an @, add *Email:* at the beginning". The required expressions are shown in **FIGURE 1**. The expression used here to find the beginning of a paragraph that contains an @ is indeed as simple as **^(.+@)**. To insert *Email:* at the beginning, simply use it as the replacement text followed by **$1**, which stands for whatever was captured by the part of the search expression in parentheses, which is in each case the text from the paragraph start up to and including the @.

You can see this in the highlighted part in the document in **FIGURE 1**. The figure shows that we've done the first address and are about to change the second one. We'll not go into the details right now; the rest of the text will make clear what happens here (briefly, ^ stands for "beginning of paragraph", and .+@ says "one or more (+) of any character (.) up to and including an @"). As I said, the details will become clear later in the text; the point of the example is to show that short and simple expressions can achieve a lot.

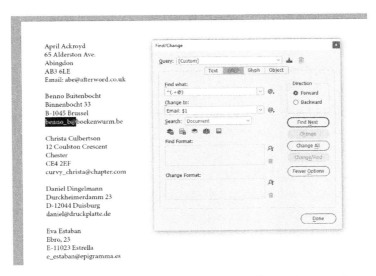

FIGURE 1. Adding text to a paragraph depending on its contents

2

The Basics: The Find/Change Dialog

Before turning to GREP expressions, it may be useful to outline the interface, which is shown in the screenshot in **FIGURE 2**. The GREP dialog is similar to the Text dialog, and virtually everything said here about GREP's dialog also holds for the Text dialog. The GREP dialog has several components, marked A to G in **FIGURE 2**. We'll deal with their contents in turn.

A. Everything you enter in the dialog (the "query") can be saved to disk for future use: search and replace strings, whether footnotes should be included, format settings – all these things are stored when you save a query and reinstated when a saved query is retrieved later. To save a query, click ⬇ (to the right of the query field) and enter a name.

B. Here you enter what you want to search for. This field accepts text, including GREP codes, though many of these can also be entered using a flyout menu. Click @, to access it. The menu is shown in **FIGURE 2**. For us, the last two sections in the menu are especially important (from Wildcards to Posix), and we'll deal with them extensively in this text. (The menu is incomplete; see

6

http://www.kahrel.plus.com/indesign/grep_classes. html for an alternative menu that lists all wildcards.)

FIGURE 2. The GREP tab of the Find/Change dialog box

Non-ASCII characters can be entered by their Unicode values. If you type, say, <014B>, that code is immediately replaced in the dialog with its character representation. If your screen font doesn't contain that character, an open square is displayed as a placeholder. This is not particularly helpful, but there is a workaround to keep the code value visible: `\x{014B}`. Use this format, and it will remain as you typed it.

You can also use a character's Unicode name. Thus, in addition to `\x{014B}` you can use the character's name in this format: `\N{Latin small letter eng}`. This format is valid for all Unicode characters, including the familiar ones such as `\N{Latin small letter e with acute}` and `\N{latin capital letter a with ogonek}`. This format is case-insensitive, so the latter is equivalent to `\N{Latin Capital Letter A with Ogonek}`, but they match case-sensitively. So the last two search patterns match only Ą. The names of all Unicode characters can be found at *www.unicode.org/charts/*.

The trouble with the field where you enter a GREP expression is that it is so small. For a more spacious environment, see *www.kahrel.plus.com/indesign/grep_editor. html*.

C. This field is used to specify the replacement text. It has its own menu, and it too is accessed by clicking @, next to the field.

D. A drop-down menu to pick the scope of the GREP: Document, All Documents, Story, To End of Story, or, if anything is selected, Selection.

E. The five symbols can be selected in any combination to specify further the search to include or exclude, from left to right, locked layers, locked stories, hidden layers, master pages, and footnotes. Note that the GREP dialog has two items fewer than the Text dialog, namely Case Sensitive and Whole Word. These two features are set using special codes in the GREP search pattern. We discuss these later.

F. In Find Format you define yet further restrictions on what the search should return. Here you specify paragraph and character styles, font settings, spacing – most formatting codes that can be set in InDesign can be searched as well. To set a formatting code, click anywhere on the panel and select from one of several subdialogs displayed (see **FIGURE 3**). The selected for-matting codes are shown in the panel (see **FIGURE 4**). When any formatting is set, a small icon, **❶**, is dis-played above the Find What and/or Change To fields. To clear the Find Format panel, click the little trash bin at the lower right.

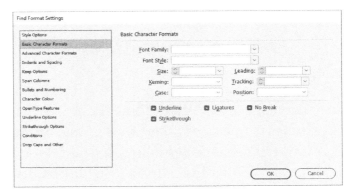

FIGURE 3. Settings for finding formatting

FIGURE 4. A query that changes formatting

G. Then, in Change Format, you set the formatting for the replacement text. With GREP searches as with text searches, you can use this panel to add or remove formatting. Some examples follow. As with the Find Format panel, if you set any formatting in Change Format, a small icon is shown above the Change to field; see **FIGURE 4** for an example. Click the trash bin to clear the formatting area and remove this icon.

Adding formatting and styling

To show how to add formatting to some text, we turn again to the GREP expression to find acronyms and apply a smallcaps style to words of two or more capitals: we've seen the GREP expression for this one earlier, and here it is shown in the interface together with the applied style (see **FIGURE 4**). The GREP expression to find acronyms is \u\u+. To apply a style to what is matched by this expression, click anywhere in the Change Format panel and set the required style. Here we selected the previously defined character style "smallcaps". Note that you leave the Change To field empty; because a style is specified in the Change Format field, the found text is not removed. Click Find and Change a few times to do some manual replacements to make sure that the query works as you intended; then click Change All to make all replacements.

A different kind of example is one that replaces one kind of formatting with another – for example, underline with italics (see **FIGURE 5**).

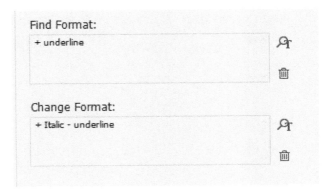

FIGURE 5. Finding and changing formatting

To get this result, you need to find underlining and replace it with not-underlining and italics. To set the search for underlining, click in the Find Format area and pick Basic Character Formats. Turn on the checkbox at Underline. Click OK to apply this setting. Now click in Change Format panel and go to Basic Character Formats again; turn off the Underline checkbox, then choose italics in the Font Style drop-down. Click OK to apply these settings as well. The applied formats are shown in the Find and Change Format panels.

Click Change All to replace all instances of underlining (again, preferably after testing).

Undocumented Features

Special GREP characters – such as wildcards – can be entered using the @, flyout menus shown earlier in **FIGURE 2**. But there are quite a few GREP sequences and features that are not listed in the flyout. I point out several of these in this guide. If you are familiar with other implementations of GREP and know of features that you can't find in InDesign's flyouts, just try and see if they work here – they often do.

3

Wildcards (or Character Classes)

Wildcards are one of the main features of GREP. The most important ones are listed in the next-to-last panel in the Find What flyout at Wildcards, though there are additional ones below at Modifiers and Posix.

A whole class of wildcards that can't be picked in the interface at all are the so-called Unicode properties. We'll illustrate the main ones along with other wildcards; see "When to optimise" on page 99 for a full overview. Finally, you can create your own wildcards by defining character classes, and this, too, will be illustrated.

Any character

As its name says, this wildcard matches anything. Its symbol is . (a dot). Enter a dot in the Find What field; clicking Find repeatedly finds each successive character in the document. The only exception is the return character (or paragraph mark), though this can be changed (see the section entitled "When to optimise" on page 99). Example: **b..d** finds all instances of four letters starting with a *b* and ending with a *d*. (**Bug:** the dot does not match footnote markers; see the troubleshooting section on page 103 for a workaround.)

Any upper-case letter

\u finds any upper-case letter. This covers all Unicode characters that can be considered letters, such as all Latin letters with accents, Cyrillic, Hebrew, and Arabic letters. I'll reintroduce our "one or more" operator, +, from page 5, as it gives more sense to the wildcards outlined in this section. \u+ means "find at least one upper-case letter". When you try it, you'll see that InDesign finds any sequence of one or more capital letters, so this simple expression is useful for finding acronyms and other abbreviations. But it also finds single-letter words such as *A* and *I*, so use \u\u+ to find sequences of two or more capitals.

Any lower-case letter

\l (lower-case L) finds any lower-case letter. As with upper-case letters, this covers all Unicode letters. It is useful that you can distinguish upper- and lower-case letters. For example, \u\l+ finds all words that begin with a capital letter.

Any letter

The expression [\u\l] doesn't distinguish upper- and lower- case letters. It is not strictly speaking a wildcard, but a character class combining the two wildcards \u and \l. We'll deal with character classes shortly.

Any digit

\d finds the digits *0* to *9*. \d+ finds all numbers consisting of one or more digits. \d also finds stylistic variants such

as old-style figures, superiors, nominators, denomina-
tors, and digits defined in non-Latin script fonts such
as Chinese and Arabic. It finds fractions constructed by
applying the Fraction feature from the character panel,
but not fractions entered by their Unicode value; ¼, when
entered as the Unicode character 00BC, is not matched
by \d; it is in fact matched only by the . wildcard and by
\p{other_number}.

Any word character

The wildcard \w matches upper- and lower-case letters,
the digits 0–9, and the underscore character. It combines
\u, \l, and \d, adding the underscore character.

Accented letters

Accented characters can be represented in two ways in
Unicode: as a single character, such as š (Unicode 0161),
or as two characters, such as s followed by a combining
diacritical ˇ: Unicodes 0073 (the s) and 030C (the ˇ).
Single characters such as Unicodes 0161 and 0073 are
matched by \u, \l, and \w, naturally, but combining diacritics are not. Thus, if the š is entered as s plus combining ˇ,
\w matches just the s. However, there is a special wildcard
to match these diacritics: \X. In fact, \X matches any single
character followed by any number of combining diacritics:
when o.ˇ is entered as o followed by Unicodes 0306 and
0323 (underdot and breve, respectively), \X matches the
combination of these three characters.

Accented letters: character equivalents

A useful wildcard from the Posix flyout (Posix stands for
Portable Operating System Interface, a system developed
to ensure the portability of programs) is the Posix character equivalent, represented in the Find What flyout menu
as [[=a=]]. In it you can place any letter between the equal
signs. [[=a=]] finds all "equivalents" of a, namely á, à, å,
ā, ã, ą. [[=z=]] matches z, ž, ź, and ż. (It is of course not
correct to say that e and é are equivalent, but we'll stick
with InDesign's usage.) Unfortunately, character equivalents are case-insensitive. This means that if you replace
[[=Ź=]] with Z, all lower-case instances, ź, are replaced
with Z, too. When you use the Posix feature, therefore,
you must always replace interactively.

Posix character equivalents are useful for replacing
possible misspellings of a name. For example, to replace
Lukacs and *Lukàcs* with *Lukács*, enter Luk[[=a=]]cs in the
Find What field and Lukács in the Change To field, then
select Story or Document and click Change All.

Finding dots and backslashes

The dot matches any character in the searched text.
But what do you do if you want to match a real dot?
The answer is that you have to "escape" it, which
you do by preceding it with an escape code, which
for InDesign GREP is a backslash. Thus \. matches
periods in a text. Backslashes, too, need to be escaped
if you want to find them in a document. To find
\fonts, use \\fonts.

Negation of wildcards with their upper-case versions
Not documented in the Wildcards flyout is that the
upper-case version of the wildcards negates them.
Thus, \D finds everything that's not a digit; \U finds
everything that's not an upper-case letter; \S matches
everything that's not white space, etc. Unicode properties, too, can be negated like this: \p{Punctuation}
matches any punctuation, \P{Punctuation} matches
everything that's not punctuation.

Digraphs

Digraphs such as *ae* in *aerogram* and *ss* in *Strasse*
are matched by [[.ae.]] and [[.ss.]]. This format matches
digraphs only when they're written as two separate letters,
so [[.ae.]] doesn't match æ, nor does [[.ss.]] match ß. It
is true of course that any occurrence of *ae* is matched
by the simple expression ae, but there are circumstances
where digraphs need to be treated as single characters;
see the discussion following "Homemade Wildcards:
Character Classes". InDesign recognizes the following
digraphs: *ae, Ae, AE, ch, Ch, CH, ll, Ll, LL, ss, Ss, SS, nj,
Nj, NJ, dz, Dz, DZ, lj, Lj, LJ*. That *oe, Oe,* and *OE* aren't
included looks like an omission.

Any whitespace

\s finds all InDesign's spaces: the space character, en
and em spaces, and all the thin spaces (thin, half, quar-
ter, etc.). It also includes tabs and returns ("paragraph
marks"). To find all sequences of spaces and tabs, use \s+ or

\p{space_separator} (or its abbreviated form \p{zs}), which matches all white space except tab and return.

Any dash

The Unicode wildcard \p{dash_punctuation} finds all dashes and hyphens.

Quotation marks

The wildcards for quotation marks are in a separate section of the flyout menu: Quotation Marks. Here you find symbols for several types of quote. "Any Double Quotation Marks" (") finds curly and noncurly quotation marks, including «guillemets» and other quote variants. Don't be misled by "Apostrophe" following "Any Single Quotation Mark", as this finds other single-quote variants such as single guillemets ‹ and ›. As both of these options specify some single or double mark, there is not a single wildcard for any quotation mark, but that's easily over-come by specifying a character class [' "] (see below for character classes), containing the single and the double straight-quote wildcard.

If a distinction between opening and closing quotes is desired, this may be attained by use of the Unicode charac-ter classes \p{initial_punctuation} and \p{final_punctuation}. They can be used in their abbreviated forms \p{pi} and \p{pf}, respectively; see the Quick Reference at the end of this guide for a complete overview.

Remember that the shape of the quotation mark you type in a document is determined by the language set in the document. Therefore the shape of quotes entered by a Find/Change query, too, is determined by the selected language. This in turn means that if you want to change English-style quotation marks ("English") to German-style („German"), all you need to do is to replace " with ", in other words, replace it with itself. (Make sure that you set the type of quotation mark in the Preferences mark in the Preferences (Edit > Preferences > Dictionary.)

Any punctuation

`[[:punct:]]` matches any punctuation: dots and commas, dashes and hyphens, braces, brackets, parentheses, all quotation marks, etc. This is a Posix wildcard, and like character equivalents, it must be entered as a character class. It can be combined with other wildcards, literals, and markers. For example, use `~F[[:punct:]]` to find foot-note markers (`~F`) followed by any punctuation. (In this case you might want to set the find options to ignore footnotes to make sure you find note numbers only in the text, not in the footnotes themselves.)

Opening and closing punctuation

`\p{open_punctuation}` finds all opening brackets, braces, and parentheses. Its abbreviated form is `\p{ps}`. The wildcard `\p{close_punctuation}` (or its short form `\p{pe}`) matches all closing brackets, braces, and parentheses. Keep in mind that quotation marks are not included in this class (see above).

Homemade wildcards: character classes

A useful feature with which you can create your own wildcards is the character class. Character classes are defined simply by listing any literal characters or wildcards enclosed in square brackets. Adobe included one in the Wildcards flyout, `[\u\l]`, to match any letter. Individual characters can be used, as can wildcards and ranges. Another example is: `[aeiouy]` which is a homemade wildcard to find (unaccented) vowels.

You can use character classes just like any other character. For instance, if you want to know if a text contains any word with two letters x with a vowel in between, search for `x[aeiouy]x`.

Posix elements, too, can be included in character classes. To match any vowel and all accented variants, use: `[[=a=][=e=][=i=][=o=][=u=][=y=]]`

In the EU headquarters, the latter formulation with equivalents will be used to match vowels; the shorter version, `[aeiouy]`, would be good for English texts only!

Here are some more examples of character classes:

`[a-z]`

The characters from a to z. A hyphen between two characters is interpreted to indicate a range. `[0-9]` matches all digits and is the equivalent of `\d`.

`[-\w]`

Earlier we saw that `\w`, "any word character", matches upper- and lower-case letters, the digits 0 to 9, and the underscore character. Crucially, it does not include the hyphen, which in many cases is indeed a word character,

20

occurring in many compounds and in names. By using [-\w] instead of \w, you work around this. [-\w]+ finds all words, including those with a hyphen, such as compounds and double-barrelled names. When you define a character class to include a hyphen, you must put that hyphen as the first character so that it can never be interpreted as indicating a range. Thus, [a-z] matches 26 letters (all letters from a to z), [-az] matches just three characters: -, a, and z.

Finding square brackets

Square brackets, like other characters that have a special meaning in GREP, must be escaped if you want to find them. Thus, to match a digit in square brackets, use \[\d\].

[\x{0400}-\x{04FF}]

Any character in the Unicode range 0400 to 04FF (Cyrillic). This is useful for assigning certain fonts or character styles to certain ranges of characters. To apply a Cyrillic font to Cyrillic characters in a text, enter the above character class in the Find What field, make sure that the Change To field is empty, and specify any formatting in Change Format. The example here finds individual Cyrillic characters; to find words in Cyrillic, simply add a +: [\x{0400}-\x{04FF}]+. If you want to find stretches of text in Cyrillic, add punctuation and the space character (\x{20}) to the character class together with anything else you need to recognise Cyrillic texts: [\x{0400}-\x{04FF}[:punct:]\x{20}]+. You may need to experiment a bit to get the character class properly defined.

Character classes, then, are flexible and easily changed. Here are some more examples:

[\d,.]+

Matches digits, commas, and period, so this expression finds numbers with decimals and thousand separators.

[£$¥\x{20A0}-\x{20CF}0-9.,]+

Matches any money amount with prefixed denomination: the currency symbols sterling, dollar, and yen; Unicode range 20A0–20CF (currency, but excludes sterling, dollar, and yen, which is why we listed them separately); and the digits 0–9, the period, and comma for decimals and thousand separator. (Note that dots needn't be escaped in character classes.)

Finally, digraphs can be used in character classes as well. To match characters in the range *ch* up to and including *g*, use this character class:

[[.ch.]-g]

This matches *ch*, *d*, *e*, *f*, and *g*, but not the single letters *c* and *h*.

Negative character classes

We saw earlier that most wildcards can be negated by changing their case: \w matches any word character, and \W matches anything that is not a word character. Character classes, too, can be negated. To find all characters that are not vowels, use [^aeiouy]. The negating element is ^, and note that it has the whole class in its scope, not just the character following it. To negate a character, you must use it in a character class. For example, to find the word *Table* when it is not followed by a digit, use Table [^\d]. Later we'll see that there are more flexible ways of achieving the same result, especially for replacing text, but for now these negative character classes are fine. An important application of negative character classes is shown in the section "Shortest match or negative character class?" on page 33.

Alternatives: Sort of a wildcard

GREP can find from among a number of alternatives. This feature is not really a wildcard, but it fits here better than anywhere else. An example with alternatives is:

(Figure|Table|Map)\s\d

This expression matches *Figure*, *Table*, and *Map* when these words are followed by a digit. Alternatives are separated by vertical bars, and all alternatives are enclosed in parentheses. The order in which you list the alternatives is often significant. Take the expression fig|figure. In a text containing both *fig* and *figure*, *figure* is never found because the expression always finds *fig* first. To ensure that you find both *fig* and *figure*, use the expression figure|fig. Thus, when alternatives partially overlap, place the longer one first.

A list with single-character alternatives is equivalent to a character class. The two expressions gr[ea]y and gr(e|a)y therefore have the same result; both match *grey* and *gray*. Though the search results are the same, Friedl[2] notes that character classes are more efficient than alternatives. Efficiency plays an important role in the design of GREP styles; see "GREP Styles" on page 89

2   Jeffrey E.F. Friedl, *Mastering Regular Expressions*, O'Reilly

Locations

InDesign GREP recognises seven find locations, though the interface includes only five (see **FIGURE 6**). The first three of these are used to get the equivalent of Whole Word in a Text search:

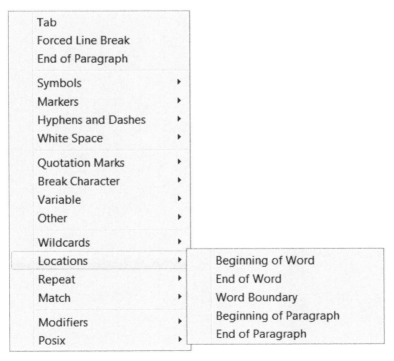

FIGURE 6. GREP locations supported by the interface

\<   Beginning of word. Example: `\<under` finds all instances of *under* at the beginning of a word. All the location matchers can be combined with wild-cards. For instance, to find all words that begin with *under*, use `\<under[-\w]+`. This formulation ensures that we find hyphenated words as well (*under-age, under-the-counter*).

Finding parentheses

(and) have a special meaning in GREP, namely, to group items. To find parentheses in a document – in other words, to find the literals – you must escape them with the backslash. We saw this earlier for the dot, the backslash itself, and the square bracket. Expressions with many escaped characters become difficult to read. For instance, to find the literal text (.*), you need to escape each character because each has a special meaning in GREP. The result is `\(\.\*\)`, which makes even the steadiest heads swim. To keep such expressions more readable, use the special symbols `\Q` and `\E`, between which everything is inter-preted literally. That impossible expression can then be given as `\Q(.*)\E`, which is much friendlier.

\>   End of word. Example: `stand\>` finds any occur-rence of *stand* at the end of a word. To match whole words that end in *stand*, use `\w+stand\>`. Note that since `\w+` means "at least one character", the word *stand* is not found, which is correct if you want to search for words that end in it. Later we'll see how to include the whole-word *stand* as well.

\b   Word boundary. This covers both beginning and end of word. This means that \<cat\> and \bcat\b are equivalent. With \< and \>, there's no real need for \b; it's there probably for compatibility reasons.

\B   Not word boundary. Searching for \Bunder\B finds *under* in *thundering* but not in *understand* and *blunder*.

^   Beginning of paragraph. Example: ^\d finds all paragraphs that start with a digit. Note that when ^ is used at the beginning of a character class, it is interpreted as negation; outside a character class, it stands for beginning of paragraph. Thus, ^[^\s]+ matches all non-space characters from the beginning of a paragraph: the first ^ is the beginning-of-paragraph marker; the second one, inside the brackets, is the negative-class marker. The beginning-of-paragraph marker can be combined with wildcards: ^\d+\.?\s finds all paragraphs that begin with a number followed (optionally, see the ? operator, below) by a dot, followed by white space.

$ End of paragraph. Example: [^.]$ finds all paragraphs that do not end in a period. \s+$ finds paragraphs with trailing white space (spaces, tabs, en and em-spaces, etc.). Note that $ is not the same as \r, the paragraph mark: $ is a location, \r is a character.

\A Beginning of story. Repeatedly searching this character cycles you through all stories in a document.

\z End of story (exceptionally, \Z has the same effect). These last two wildcards, when combined as \A\z, find empty text frames: if a text frame contains the beginning of a story directly followed by the end of a story, that story is empty, and its containing text frame is therefore also empty. This works only for unthreaded text frames.

It is important that you realise that these GREP characters match locations, not characters. You can see this by the result of a search. Use \d to find a digit, and you'll see that the first found digit is selected. Search \r, the paragraph mark, and you see that that mark (the hard-return character, in fact) is selected. On the other hand, search $ to find the end of a paragraph, and nothing is selected: the cursor is placed at the end of the first found paragraph, but there is no selection.

It is interesting that we can find these locations, as they allow us to add things at the beginning or end of words, paragraphs, and stories. But we need to cover some more ground before we can deal with that; we'll return to this in "Replacing using location markers" on page 82.

Repeat: Sequence of Characters

Without GREP, to replace sequences of space characters with just a single space, you had to repeatedly replace two spaces with one until there were no more double spaces left. GREP makes this much simpler; search any sequence of two or more spaces and replace them with a single one: find \x{20}\x{20}+ and replace with \x{20}. As we've seen earlier, the plus is a repeat character and means "at least once", so that the expression paraphrases as "find a space followed by a sequence of at least one space". There are several repeat characters; they're all in the Repeat flyout (see **FIGURE 7**). We'll deal with them in turn.

? Zero or one time

To find, say, both British and American spellings *harbour* and *harbor*, search for harbou?r. The scope of ? is just one character, so in this example it applies only to the *u*. The expression paraphrases as "find *harbo*, perhaps followed by *u* (or, followed by zero or one occurrence of *u*), followed by *r*". To extend the scope of ? to more characters, group them with parentheses: (19)?\d\d finds all two-digit numbers (matched by \d\d), as well as four-digit numbers whose first two digits are *19*. You can combine this with alternation: `(18|19|20)?\d\d` matches two-digit numbers as well as four-digit numbers that begin with *18, 19,* or *20.*

The `?` operator is useful for matching numbers as well – for example, in dates. The expression `\d\d-\d\d-\d\d\d\d` finds dates formatted like *08-04-2018.* But dates come in different shapes, so to allow for single-digit days and months and double-digit years, as in *8-12-18,* use `\d\d?-\d\d?-(\d\d)?\d\d`.

FIGURE 7. Repeat options

* Zero or more times

Search `\w*` and any sequence of word characters will be found, including no word characters! This operator needs

to be handled with care. Try using the + operator when-ever possible (see the next section). Like ?, the scope of *
is just one character, so group any characters with paren-theses to extend its scope.

+ One or more times

Similar to the * operator. The difference is that there must be at least one match. To find all words in upper-case letters, use the search string \u+. Try using this operator rather than * whenever you can because it's more effi-cient. In this example it's nonsensical to use \u*; we're interested in its occurrence so we don't want to try and match where it does not occur.

The operators here can be combined with character classes, too. [aeiouy]+ finds any sequence of vowels. For example, to find all words in a text that begin with *b*, end in *t*, and have any number of vowels between the *b* and the *t*, use \bb[aeiou]+t\b. This finds *bat, bet, bit, but, boat, beaut*, etc.

The last three repeat operators in **FIGURE 7** (Shortest Match) are dealt with together in the next section.

Shortest match: lazy operators

Say you want to find text between double quotation marks. Your first shot would probably be ".+". But you'll soon find that this expression is over-enthusiastic, or in GREP-speak, greedy. This is an apt description as the *
and + operators try to consume as much text as possible. That's why, in a text like this:

"Bother!" said Pooh. "It all comes of trying to be kind to Heffalumps."

the expression matches from the first opening quotation mark to the last closing quotation mark, finding, therefore, one instance. That's the + operator's greedy behaviour, and it's clearly not what you want. To reign in the operator's greed, tell it to use not the longest match, but the shortest one: ".+?" – in other words, the operator should become lazy. The reformulation, therefore, finds both occurrences. (Sometimes we want + and * to be greedy; see page 56.)

Alternative: Negative character class

An alternative to using ? to restrict the scope of * and + is to use a negative character class. Our earlier expression ".+?" can be recast as one using a negative character class as follows: "[^"]+", which translates as "start at a double quotation mark, one or more characters (+) which are not a quotation mark ([^"]) to the first next quotation mark. In this expression, [^"] is the negative character class.

Making expressions easier to read

Expressions can be made clearer by adding spaces and comments. Take this expression:

\w+([lst])(ed|ing)

which would be a bit easier to read if you add some spaces. To do so, add (?x) – the undocumented "free spacing" modifier – at the beginning of the expression:

(?x)   \w+   ([lst])   (ed|ing)

which lets you make it more readable. In this free-spacing mode, spaces are ignored, so if you want to match a space, use \x{20}, the Unicode value of the space. You could also add comments to an expression:

\w+([lst])(?# match l, s, or t)\1(?# match same letter) (ed|ing)

Anything between (?# and) is ignored. The two modes, free spacing and comments, can be combined:

(?x) \w+ ([lst])   (?# match l, s, or t)   \1   (?# match same letter)   (ed|ing)

For an even more convenient way of editing GREP expressions, in which expressions can be written on several lines, see *www.kahrel.plus.com/indesign/ grep_editor.html*.

Shortest match or negative character class?

The two methods – shortest match and negative character class – aim to achieve the same goal, namely, to consume as little text as possible. The choice for either method is determined by several factors.

First, negative character classes tend to be quicker than lazy operators because the lazy operator, in order to find the shortest match, in fact needs to find all matches after which it selects the shortest match (it "backtracks"). Negative character classes don't backtrack, therefore have less overhead, and are therefore preferred. But unfortunately, you can't always use them. Suppose you want to match text wrapped in HTML-like codes, as in the following example:

Tedious examples such as <i>the quick brown fox</i> jumped over <i>the lazy dog</i> bore your readers.

The GREP expression `<i>[^<]+</i>` finds each stretch of text in between the codes <i> and </i>. That's what we want. But this works only as long as there's no intervening code < in the text. Thus, the expression doesn't work in this example:

Repeating boring examples such as <i>the quick <b>brown</b> fox jumped over the lazy dog</i> will annoy your readers.

Because there's a code <b> intervening between the opening <i> and the closing </i>, our expression doesn't find anything in this example. We're forced to use the lazy-operator method, `<i>.+?</i>`.

On the other hand, the negative character class approach is required when you try to match texts like this at the end of a paragraph; see the example on matching paragraph-final parentheticals on page 85.

Repeating a pattern a specific number of times

There are some repeat operators that are not included in the interface – I assume because of an oversight, for they are quite useful:

{n}   Match **exactly** n times. For example, \b\w{4}\b finds all four-letter words (\b identifies word boundaries, \w matches letters and digits) ; ^([\S]+\s){3} matches the first three words of a paragraph (^ is the start of the paragraph; [\S]+ matches any sequence of non-spaces to the first space \s; {3} three times).

{n,}   Match **at least** n times. \b\d{6,} matches all numbers of six digits or more.

{n, p}   Match **between** n and p times (inclusive). \b\w{4,7}\b finds all words between four and seven characters long.

6

Referring to Wildcards: Back-Referencing

We have seen that we can find, say, words that contain two consecutive vowels; the expression \w*[aeiouy] [aeiouy]\w* does that. This finds words like *tough*, *blood*, *clear*, and *too*. But what if we want to find words with two consecutive identical vowels, so that we find *blood* and *too*, but not *lead* and *tea*? What we're after is something like "Find a word with a vowel followed by that same vowel". This is possible in a GREP expression:

\w*([aeiouy])\1\w*

The expression is analyzed as follows:

\w*	any word characters
([aeiouy])	capture any vowel
\1	match that same vowel
\w*	any word characters

The expression differs from the first one (\w*[aeiouy] [aeiouy]\w*) in two respects. First, the vowel wildcard is in parentheses. Like earlier examples of parentheses, they group something – even though the group consists of just one element, namely a character class. But apart from that, the parentheses also create a referent – that is, something that can be referred to. Referrers are numbers preceded by a backslash (the backslash is an escape character here to distinguish the referrer from a normal digit). In the example, \1 refers to the first parenthetical, and it assumes the identity of whatever vowel precedes it.

What counts as a group for back references?

Modifiers such as the free-space modifier (?x) and comments (?#) are ignored in the back-reference count. Thus, (?x) (\u) \1 is equivalent to (\u)\1: \1 refers to \u in both cases.

A similar example is the search pattern to try to match words like *travelling*, *focussed*, and *formatting* – that is, verbs that double their final consonant when used in the past tense or as a present participle. The expression to find these verb forms is the following:

\w+([lst])\1(ed|ing)\b

This expression is analysed as follows:

\w+	one or more word characters
([lst])	one of the letters l, s, or t
\1	the same letter (l, s, or t)
(ed|ing)	*ed* or *ing*
\b	at the word boundary (in this case, the end of the word)

This expression, then, finds *l*, *s*, and *t* followed by the same letter – so we match *ll*, *ss*, and *tt* – followed by *ed* or *ing*. We add \w+ at the beginning to include all word characters that precede the double consonant, and \b at the end for good measure to avoid words and names that have word characters following *ed* and *ing*, like *Dillinger*.

A special referrer: $0

$1, $2, etc. in the Change To field refer to the first, second, etc. grouped items in the "Find what" field. The special referrer $0 refers to the whole match. In ^(\w+)\s(\w+)$, the first word of the match is referred to by $1, the second word by $2. $0 refers to the whole match, i.e., both words and the space between them.

Here is another example. Earlier we saw an example to find dates:

\d\d?-\d\d?-(\d\d)?\d\d

This expression is reasonably flexible in that it allows for single- and double-digit days and months, and double- and quadruple-digit years. But still it expects the three items to be separated by a hyphen, whereas we would like to allow slashes as well. This is possible by creating character classes for the separators:

\d\d?[-/]\d\d?[-/](\d\d)?\d\d

Broken down:

\d\d?	one or two digits
[-/]	a hyphen or a slash
\d\d?	one or two digits
[-/]	a hyphen or a slash
(\d\d)?\d\d	capture two digits followed by two more digits, or match two digits

This is a bit better, but what we really want is to find *04-12-2018* and *3/9/1999*, but not *6/4-1877*, as this is not a date. To make sure we find identical separators, we create a back reference:

`(?x)  \d\d?  ([-/])  \d\d?  \1  (\d\d)?\d\d`

You can create more than one back reference in an expression. For example, to match magic dates such as *11-11-1911* and *11/11/11,* you'd need something like this:

`(\d\d?)([-/])\1\2(\d\d)?\1`

Broken down:

 `(\d\d?)` capture one or two digits

  `([-/])` capture a hyphen or a slash separator

   `\1` match what we captured in the first parenthetical (one or two digits)

   `\2` match what we captured in the second parenthetical (hyphen or slash separator)

 `(\d\d)?` match two digits or nothing

   `\1` match what we captured in the first parenthetical – those same digits

The first one or two digits are the first group, which we refer to using `\1`. Then there's the character class defining a separator, which is made into a group, too, and is referred to using `\2`. Then follows a reference to the first group (the first one or two digits in the date), stipulating that the first and the second number are identical. Now we get a reference to the second group, stipulating that the second separator is identical to the first one. Finally, we may get any two digits `(\d\d)?`, followed by another back reference to the first number of the string. Note that `(\d\d)?`, too, creates a referent, but here we use the parentheses only to group the two digits so that both are in the scope of ?.

7

Finding Formatted Text

In the GREP tab you can constrain the GREP expression to text with certain formatting: both local formatting and a character and/or paragraph style. For example, to find all sequences of two or more capital letters that have been formatted as small caps, use the search pattern we saw earlier, `\u\u+`, and set Small Caps in the Find Format area.

Another example: let us think how we would go about finding paragraphs formatted in bold from beginning to end. To find a whole paragraph, we need to match from its beginning to its end and match everything in between: `^.+$`

To find the paragraphs set from beginning to end in bold, simply enter this pattern, then go into Find Format and set Font Style to Bold in Basic Character Formats.

8

Replacing with Wildcards

Now that we know how to find things using GREP's wild-cards, we're ready to do some replacing with them. If the find text does not contain wildcards or references to wild-cards, the replacement is straightforward. For example, to replace the words *illustration*, *graph*, *map*, and *chart* with *figure*, do this:

Find what: illustration|graph|map|chart
Change to: figure

The words that should be replaced are given as a list of alternatives separated by the vertical bar, and each alter-native is replaced with *figure*. GREP is case-sensitive by default; to replace case-insensitively, it is necessary to add (?i) before the expression. This will replace *chart* with *figure* and *Chart* with *Figure*.

This kind of replacement is already a great leap for-ward compared with the replacements you can do in the Text tab. By including wildcards and references to them, GREP replacements become really powerful. Let's look at some applications of this.

Swap first and last name

Suppose you have a list of names of people, one person per line, the first name followed by the last name:

> Zack Adams
>
> Yolanda Brolin
>
> Xaviera Cummings
>
> etc.

(We assume in this case that every person has just one first name and one last name.) Now you want to change that list so that the last name comes first, followed by a comma, followed by a space and the first name:

> Adams, Zack
>
> Brolin, Yolanda
>
> Cummings, Xaviera
>
> etc.

We saw earlier that a single word, if unhyphenated, is matched by \w+. Two words on a line are matched by ^\w+\s\w+$: a word (\w+) at the beginning of a paragraph (^) and one at the end ($) with a space (\s) between them. In order to refer to these words later, we add parentheses to each of them. The required expressions to swap the words are:

Find what: ^(\w+)\s(\w+)$

Change to: $2, $1

Broken down:

> $2 insert the second parenthetical (the surname)
>
> , insert a comma and a space
>
> $1 insert the first parenthetical (the first name)

The first group in the find expression (the first names) is referred to by $1 in the change expression, the second one (the last names) by $2. You can use up to nine back references ($1 to $9). To swap the first and last name, simply use a reference to the second group before the reference to the first one, as shown. Any other text in the Change To field is entered literally, and there's no need to escape anything: the dollar symbol is the only special GREP character in the Change To field.

Strictly speaking, it isn't necessary to include ^ and $ – after all, \w matches just word characters, so the expression also works without these beginning-of- and end-of-paragraph markers. However, if you leave them out and you have the cursor somewhere in the text, the match for the selected paragraph starts at the cursor position, not at the beginning of that paragraph. Another reason to add those markers is that they make the expression more explicit for InDesign, making it more efficient and thus probably quicker.

The expression given above, though correct, is hopelessly inadequate. It doesn't deal with initials followed by a period, nor does it recognise double-barrelled (hyphenated) names. To remedy that, use the following Find What expression (the "Change to" expression remains the same):

Find what: ^([-\w.]+)\s([-\w.]+)$

Broken down:

    ^ beginning of paragraph

([-\w.]+) one or more of hyphen, word character, and/or period

\s any white space

([-\w.]+) once more, one or more of hyphen, word character, and/or period

$ end of paragraph marker

We define here a character class [-\w.] to capture any character that can be part of a name, which is the word character (i.e. any letter), the hyphen (to capture hyphenated names), and the dot (to capture initials – that is, word characters followed by dots).

Swap last name and initials in a selection

For our next example we'll look at changing things in a selection, again using something that often needs to be replaced in a bibliography. A frequent change is moving initials before the last name – in other words, changing *Fodor, J. A.* to *J. A. Fodor*. It's not really possible to apply an expression to a whole bibliography in one go, because there are often too many things that resemble names but aren't. So what we can do is select the name and the initials, and use the following expressions on that selection:

Find what: ([-\w]+),\s(.+)

Change to: $2 $1

The last name is captured by [-\w+], which includes all characters from the beginning of the selection up to the comma. The comma and the following space are matched but since we leave them outside parentheses, they're not captured. Then we capture the initials simply by capturing everything after the space until the end of the selection – there's no need to try and define precisely what initials are since we're selecting manually. The replacement is made simply by stating that what is captured first comes after what is captured second. Make sure that the scope of the replacement is Selection – not All Documents, Document, Story, or To End of Story – and click Change.

Change first names to initials

We could do more with the name list. Suppose you want to change all first names to initials followed by a dot. (Again, for simplicity, we assume that the list has two words on each line, a first name followed by a last name.) To change each first name to its initial, do this:

Find what: ^(\u)\l+
Change to: $1.

First note that we don't need the last name at all: we're interested only in the first word of each line/paragraph, which is the first name. Of this first name, we want to keep only the initial upper-case letter (\u); we don't care about the following lower-case letters, matched by \l, which is why we don't capture them in parentheses. So all we need to do is to change what we've found with a reference to the first group and add a period. By saying that the initial capital letter should be followed by at least one lower-case letter, we ensure that first names that are already in the form of an initial are not affected.

Unfortunately, the formulation here doesn't handle hyphenated first names such as *Jean-Louis* and *Ying-Ting*. *Jean-Louis*, for example, is changed to *J.-Louis*. To deal with these, we need to change both the find and the change expressions:

Find what: `^(\u)\l+(-\u)\l+`
Change to: `$1.$2.`

Broken down:

`^`	Beginning of paragraph
`(\u)\l+`	Uppercase letter followed by one or more lower-case letters (capture the capital)
`(-\u)\l+`	Hyphen and upper-case letter followed by one or more lower-case letters (capture the hyphen and the capital)

This replaces *Jean-Louis* with *J.-L.* But now we don't match single first names like *James* any longer. Can we not reconcile the two Find/Change pairs and come up with one set of expressions that deals with both types of first name? Unfortunately, we can't. As we need different "Change to" expressions, we have to change the two types of first name in two different change operations.

However, using two (or even more) operations in succession isn't a big problem: just save each operation as a separate query and use a script to chain the queries. See "Chaining GREP Queries" on page 61 for details.

Change date format

In the next example, returning to the dates that we used earlier, we'll again see nested references. Let's first see what we had. We saw that this:

`(?x)   \d\d?   ([-/])   \d\d?   \1   \d\d\d\d`

matches dates of the form *2-11-2018* and *15/1/1960*. The first separator in this expression (`[-/]`) was placed in parentheses so that it could be referred to. `\1` is the refer-rer in the find expression (this can be used in the change expression, too, as we'll see in a moment).

Let's say we want to swap the order of month and date, to switch between American and European date formats. To swap the first two numbers, we need to enclose both in parentheses. We also want the year in the replacement, so it, too, needs to be placed in parentheses. That's the general principle: everything you want to refer to needs to go in parentheses. For the moment we'll say that whatever the separator is, we'll standardise on a hyphen. Therefore, we end up with these expressions:

Find what: `(?x)   (\d\d?)   ([-/])   (\d\d?)   \2   (\d\d\d\d)`
Change to: `$3-$1-$4`

Notice first of all that since we added some groupings, the first separator is no longer the first grouping: it is now the second one, so we must use `\2` to refer to it. In the change expression, `$3` refers to the second number (`\d\d?`), `-` is the hyphen we want in the changed dates, `$1` refers to the first number (`\d\d?`), there's another separator, and finally we have `$4`, the year.

Now, if we had wanted to keep whatever separators were in the found string, all we'd need to do is modify the change string as follows:

Change to: $3$2$1$2$4

And to accommodate both double-digit and quadru-ple-digit years such as *15-1-1960* and *15-1-60*, as we did before, the first two digits of the year should be grouped and made optional:

Find what:
(?x) (\d\d?) ([-/]) (\d\d?) 2 ((\d\d)?\d\d)
Change to: $3-$1-$4

We saw earlier that in nested groupings, the encom-passing group is counted first and the nested one second. In this example, therefore, $4 refers to the third whole group, which is ((\d\d)?\d\d), and $5 refers to the nested group, (\d\d).

Remove dots at the end of section headings

You're working on a book with twenty chapters, and each chapter contains numbered sections. All section headings end in a period, and you're supposed to remove all these periods. With a GREP expression this is surprisingly easy:

Find what: ^(\d\d?\..+)\.$
Change to: $1

Broken down:
       ^ beginning of paragraph
       (start capture
  \d\d?\. one or two digits followed by a dot

.+ one or more characters
) end capture
\. dot . . .
$ . . . at the end of the paragraph

We define a section heading as a paragraph that starts with a single- or a double-digit number (\d\d?) followed by a period (\.), followed by one or more characters (.+). If we can match a period at the end of the paragraph (\.$), we know that it should be deleted ("deleted" here means that the whole paragraph is replaced with itself minus the period). Naturally, these expressions can be used automatically only when there aren't any numbered lists anywhere in the documents. But even if there are, you could still use these expressions and do the replacements interactively.

Remove duplicate entries in a list

An interesting application of GREP is the removal of duplicate entries from a sorted list. This sounds complicated, but all it takes is the following surprisingly simple expression, inspired by http://www.regular-expressions. info (\r is the paragraph mark):

Find what: ([^\r]+\r)\1+
Change to: $1

Broken down:

(start capture
[^\r]+ while not \r, continue capturing
\r include that \r
) end capture

\1+ match the capture one or more times.

Suppose you have a list that looks like this:
Leech 1998
Leech 1998
Leech 1998
Leech 2000
McCawley 1988
. . .
. . .

Remember that paragraph marks are characters like any other; that they're written with the escape character \ doesn't alter that. The expression therefore uses a negated character class (consisting here of just the paragraph mark) to find the end of a paragraph, and then includes that paragraph mark in the referenced expression. So the first match is **Leech 1998\r**. Any duplicates of this (\1+, i.e. referent followed with + operator) are replaced with the referent alone, which amounts to deleting the duplicates.

Replace certain hyphens with an en dash

En dashes (or en rules) are used frequently in Anglo-American publishing. In the following section, "Splitting Up Complex Expressions", we deal separately with the case of page ranges, which can be dealt with automatically. Here we go into compounds that can't be dealt with automatically. Consider the following examples:

French-English dictionaries
the Keenan-Comrie hypothesis
Sino-Tibetan languages

Anglo-American

According to certain style guides, in the first two examples the hyphen needs to be replaced with an en dash,
but in the last two it should not. The trouble is that you
can't predict this: all you know is that potential candidates are two words, both with an initial capital, joined
by a hyphen. But since this is an easily defined pattern,
you can formulate find-and-replace patterns and do the
replacements interactively. These are the required expressions (~= is the symbol for the en dash):

Find what: `(\u\w+)-(\u\w+)`
Change to: `$1~=$2`

The pattern `\u\w+` describes any word with an initial
capital; two of these separated by a hyphen describe the
pattern we're after.

Splitting Up Complex GREP Expressions

We've seen in some examples that GREP expressions can quickly become quite complex. One way of battling complexity is to split expressions up into separate expressions. An added benefit of splitting up expressions is that they are easier to modify. A good example of a query that benefits from splitting up is finding hyphens in ranges and replacing them with en dashes. As we will see, it's not easy to come up with a single expression to accomplish this.

Replace hyphens in page ranges with en-dashes

The ranges we're after are ranges of numbers, both Arabic and Roman (e.g. *34-78*, *v-ix*), ranges of numbers in parentheses (as in *(23)-(27)*), and certain letter ranges (*a-d*), which could be preceded by a number (as in *6b-d*). The first type, ranges of Arabic numbers such as *23-56*, can be handled with this query:

Find what: `(\d)-(\d)`
Change to: `$1~=$2`

Note that this query can be over-enthusiastic in that it changes hyphens in numbers which aren't page ranges, such as such as ISBN numbers, telephone numbers, and grant numbers. The \b location marker is of no use here because hyphens are seen as word boundaries, so an expression such as \b(\d+)-(\d+)\b matches 0-596 in 978-0-596-51706-9. This can can be avoided, but we need some extra tools for that; see "Replace hyphens in page ranges – revisited" on page 75.

Hyphens in ranges of Arabic numbers in parenthe-ses such as (12)-(14) can be captured with the following expressions:

Find what: (?x) ([\d()]+) - ([\d()]+)
Change to: $1~=$2

In order to match a number with its enclosing paren-theses, we need to define a character class containing \d, (, and). Note again that the parentheses needn't be escaped in a character class.

Hyphens in Roman page ranges such as ii-xv are replaced with an en dash as follows:

Find what: (?x) ([ivxl]+) - ([ivxl]+)
Change to: $1~=$2

To match roman digits, a class is defined consisting of i, v, x, and l. I exclude c, d, and m from the class as Roman page numbers never exceed 89, but also to avoid the risk of finding combinations with dim, mid, clic, lid, and mild – even though such combinations on both sides of the hyphen are extremely unlikely.

Finally, in ranges of single letters such as a-d, option-ally preceded by a number, as in 5b-e, the hyphen can be replaced with these expressions:

Find what: `(\d?[a-z])-([a-z])\b`
Change to: `$1~=$2`

This leaves us with four expressions, so if we have to replace hyphens we need to use four different queries, which is awkward. But looking at the first three find expressions we notice that they are pretty similar, and in fact they can be combined into one set of expressions as follows:

Find what: `(?x)  ([ivxl\d()]+)  -  ([ivxl\d()]+)`
Change to: `$1~=$2`

Though this reduces the number of queries, you still need to use two of them. Again, InDesign's interface doesn't allow you to chain queries and so they must be run one after the other. But queries can be chained using a script; see "Chaining GREP Queries" on page 61 for details.

Drop digits

Another candidate for splitting up is the regular expression for dropping digits in page ranges (also known as "abbreviating inclusive pages"), so that *34–39* is changed to *34–9*, and *123–128* to *123–8*. This is relatively straightforward, but there is a complication: namely, in English-language texts the teens aren't dropped: *12–17* should not be altered (the reason is that you can't pronounce something like *12–7*). There aren't hard-and-fast rules for dropping digits in this way; in Britain, continental Europe, Australia, and the United States, different types of abbreviation may be used. Here we aim for a type of abbreviation common in Britain, which tries to drop as many digits as possible (apart from the teens).

It turns out to be difficult to capture this in one expression, whereas it is not so hard first to include the teens to drop them too, and reinstate them later. The added advantage is that in a document using a language that does drop the teens, nothing more needs to be done. The expressions needed for the first step, dropping the digits, are the following:

Find what: (?x)   \b   (\d+)(\d+)   ~=   \1(\d+)   \b
Change to: $1$2~=$3

Broken down:

\b	word boundary
(\d+)(\d+)	one or more digits followed by one or more digits; capture them separately
~=	en rule
\1	match whatever was captured in the first parenthetical
(\d+)	one or more digits
\b	word boundary

This expression tries to find identical beginning sequences of digits left and right of the dash, deleting any such identical items on the right of the dash. Some examples: 234–239 is matched by the expression as follows:

23	4	–	23	9
(\d+)	(d+)	-	\1	\d

Note that here we make use of the greed of the + operator. Because it tries to consume as much text as it can, it matches the 23 part of 234. Had we tamed the operator, as in (\d+?)(\d+), then we would have matched just the 2 in 234.

To reinstate the teens, we need to do this:

Find what: (?x) \b (\d*1\d ~=) (?=\d\b)
Change to: $11

The find expression (which includes the "positive look-ahead" ?=; see the section entitled "Look Ahead: Match selectively" on page 67) matches the digit 1 preceded by zero or more digits and followed by another digit, fol-lowed by an en dash, a digit and a word boundary – e.g. 13–6, 215–8, and 1912–6 – and inserts a 1 after the dash. The word boundary is absolutely necessary, because without it 215–23 would be changed to 215–123.

Inserting thousand separators

Inserting thousand separators, to change 12345678 to 12,345,678 (or use any other symbol, such as a dot or a thin space) could be handled with one query (this one is from Friedl's *Mastering Regular Expressions, p. 67*):

Find what: (\d)(?=(\d\d\d)+\b)
Change to: $1,

(You can change the comma following $1 to your separator character or space of choice.) I wrote "could be handled with one query", because if the numbers you want to process are in tables, then the above expressions won't work. It's not entirely clear to me why, but I suspect it's because of the \b word-boundary code which doesn't match the \Z end-of-story code (each table cell is a separate story). To deal with numbers in tables, you could insert a thin space after each number, then insert the thousand separators, and, finally, remove the added space. (Adding spaces is harmless: even when cells become overset their contents will be processed correctly.) All this means that three queries are required:

Find what: (\d\d\d\d)\Z
Change to: $1~|
Find what: (\d)(?=(\d\d\d)+\b)
Change to: $1,
Find what: ~|\Z
Change to: <leave blank>

The first query looks for four-digit numbers (\d\d\d\d) at the end of a story (\Z) and replaces that digit with itself ($1), so to speak, and a hair space: that's the equivalent of inserting someting at a location. We look for four-digit numbers because we're not interested in shorter numbers. The second query inserts the thousand separators. The third query removes any hair spaces at the end of a story.

Keeping initials together

Bibliographies and reference lists abound in names preceded by initials that are broken at random places. A general rule is that single initials (as in G. *Leech*) should stay together with the surname, while multiple initials (*E. E. Cummings*) can stay together on one line with the sur-name on the next line. For reasons that will soon become apparent, we have to do the multiple initials first. What we'll do is find any series of initials, with 'initial' defined simply as an upper-case letter followed by a period and a space, and apply the No Break feature to them:

Find what: `\u\.(\s\u\.)+`

Change to: <leave empty>

Change format: No Break

> `\u\.` match an upper-case letter followed by a period
>
> `(` start capture
>
> `\s\u\.` any white space followed by an upper-case letter and a period
>
> `)+` end capture; capture one or more times

Note that we use `\u\.(\s\u\.)+`, not `\u\.\s(\u\.\s)+` (the difference is in including the space in the capture). The reason is that the latter applies No Break to the space between the initials and the surname, which causes initials and surname (or at any rate its first syllable) to stay together. The former formulation avoids that. (When testing expressions like these, which may not do anything immediately visible, it is useful temporarily to add something visible, such as underlining, so that you can see where exactly No Break is applied. In this example, we'd add underlining until we're satisfied that the GREP works well, then remove it.)

Turning to single initials, these, too, are handled with the No Break feature. In this case, however, we "connect" the initial to the surname. For single initials we need to search for a capital followed by a period and a space, followed either by a capital and lower-case letter (*Leech*), a capital and an apostrophe, (*O'Neill*), a capital and a space

(*Ó Baoill*), or a prefix such as *von, van, der, vander, den, de, ten, ter, te, du, la, 't, d'*, and *l'* to capture just German, Flemish, Dutch, and French name prefixes. The following expressions handle all these cases (to avoid catching the multiple initials we did earlier, we need to specify –No Break in the Find Format section):

Find what: \u\. (?i)(von |vander |van |
der |den |de |ten |ter |te |du |la |'t |
d'|l'|\u)*\u(\l|'\u| \u)*

Find format: –No Break (i.e. deselect No Break)
Change to: <leave empty>
Change format: No Break

The list of possible prefixes must be modified by * to capture names that don't have any prefixes, and names that have multiple prefixes such as *J. de la Fontaine* and *G. von der Gabelentz*. Finally, note that we added (?i) to match any prefixes case-insensitively. This is necessary to match Flemish names such as *Vander Meesteren* and prefixed names in North America, such as *R. Van Valin*.

The list of alternatives could be condensed as follows, which makes it shorter but does nothing for readability:

(v[oa]n |[td]e[nr]? |vander? |du |la |'t |[dl]'|\u)

The first alternative, v[oa]n, matches *von* and *van*; the second, [td]e[nr]?, *te, ten, ter, de, den, der*; vander? matches *vande* and *vander*; the others need no comment.

10

Chaining GREP Queries

We've seen that it is often preferable, and sometimes even necessary, to use more than one expression to achieve something. But unfortunately it is not possible in GREP's interface to chain two or more expressions, so you may find yourself running saved queries in succession.

However, you can chain queries using a simple script, so that any number of queries can be executed by running a single script. Here's an example. Let's say you saved the three queries needed to add thousand separators in three queries and that you called those queries thousand_1, thousand_2, and thousand_3. The text of the script to execute the three queries is as follows:

```
app.loadFindChangeQuery ('thousand-1',
       SearchModes.GREP_SEARCH);
app.activeDocument.changeGrep();
app.loadFindChangeQuery ('thousand-2',
       SearchModes.GREP_SEARCH);
app.activeDocument.changeGrep();
app.loadFindChangeQuery ('thousand-3',
       SearchModes.GREP_SEARCH);
app.activeDocument.changeGrep();
```

Save these lines in a plain text file, calling it, say, *thousand_separators.jsx* (the name itself is not important, but for the file extension you must use *jsx*). Place the script file in your script directory. If you don't know where that is, you can locate it as follows:

1. In InDesign, open the Scripts panel (Window > Utilities > Scripts).
2. Select the User folder in the panel, then click the flyout button ▤ (see **FIGURE 8**).
3. Select "Reveal in Explorer" (PC) or "Reveal in Finder" (Mac). This opens a window showing the script folder.
4. Copy the script file to that folder.
5. The script is shown in the Scripts panel straight away. To run the script, double-click it. The script can be used on Macs and Windows PCs.

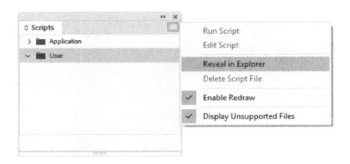

FIGURE 8. The Scripts panel

Another possibility is to use the script available at *http://www.kahrel.plus.com/indesign/chain_queries.html*. With the script you can create chains of queries and execute them. It is more flexible in its application (document, story, selection, etc.), and you can manage queries.

11

Applying Styles with GREP Find/Change

You can apply character styles automatically using GREP Styles in the Paragraph Style dialog. This is a powerful and flexible way of applying character styles, but it is often easier and/or more efficient to apply styles using the Find/Change dialog. Besides, it's not possible to apply paragraph styles using GREP styles. Here we go into applying styles using the Find/Change dialog, GREP styles are illustrated separately; see the section "GREP Styles" on page 89.

Say you have a book with numbered chapters and numbered sections, such that Chapter 1 has first-level sections 1.1, 1.2, 1.3, etc., Chapter 2 contains sections 2.1, 2.2, and so on. These sections can have subsections – second-level sections – numbered 1.1.1, 1.1.2, etc. There might be more, but let's assume that this text has two levels of section numbering. The documents you're processing have no styles applied to them at all, so you're starting from scratch. Let's say that you use paragraph style 'secA' for the first-level sections and 'secB' for the second-level ones. How can we use GREP to save us from at least part of the tedium of finding the section headings in the documents and applying the appropriate styles to them?

First we need to have an idea what those section headings in fact look like in the documents and devise an
expression that catches them all. Well, each is a series of
digits and dots, with a space between the number and the
body. While you're working on a chapter, you notice that
some sections end in a dot, others don't, and that some
have a space between number and body, others a tab, and
yet others combinations of these. It's a mess, but all these
variants are still straightforward to manage. To apply first-
level styles, do this:

Find what: `^(\d\d?)\.?\s+`
Change to: `$1.\t`
Change format: paragraph style secA

Broken down:

`^`	beginning of paragraph
`(\d\d?)`	capture one or two digits
`\.?`	possibly followed by a period
`\s+`	and one or more spaces

(You could do this interactively to be on the safe side,
or automatically if you know for certain that the expression captures just section headings.) What we do is this:
we search a start-of-paragraph marker followed by a
number that could consist of one or two digits (`\d\d?`) followed perhaps by a dot (`\.?`), which in turn is followed by
one or more spaces of any type (`\s+`). The number is captured in a group so we can refer to it in the replace string,
which in effect replaces any spaces between number
and body with a tab as the paragraph style is applied at
the same time. Note that by keeping the dot outside the

capture group we can automatically correct inconsisten-cies, as in:

Before: 1. Section a
           2 Section b

After: 1. Section a
           2. Section b

To apply the second-level styles, we use comparable expressions:

Find what: ^(\d\d?\.\d\d?)\.?\s+
Change to: $1.\t
Change format: paragraph style secB

This is just a slight variation, matching two num-bers separated by a dot at the start of a paragraph. The replacement string remains the same. The query could easily be adapted to handle deeper-level section headings. You need a separate expression for each level, though you can chain them all using the script described in the sec-tion "Chaining GREP Queries" on page 61.

If you want to use section headings with automatic paragraph numbering, you cand find the section head-ings in a document, apply the relevant auto-numbered paragraph style, and delete the number. Assuming that the secA paragraph style is defined with an appropriate numbered list, do this:

Find what: ^\d\d?\.?\s+(.)
Change to: $1
Change format: paragraph style secA

Here, (.) captures the first character of the section heading's title, and by setting the replacement string to $1 we in effect replace that first character with itself. This trick (suggested by Kai Rübsamen) forces InDesign to insert some text, so that the paragraph style is applied. If we wouldn't apply this trick, then we'd have to make two passes: one pass using ^\d\d?\.?\s+ (i.e. without the final (.)) and leaving the Change to field empty, applying the paragraph style to whatever we find; the second pass, applying the same Find What and Change To strings but without any formatting, to delete the static numbers.

Repeat the above query, modifying the find string as necessary, for any other section level.

12

Looking Around with GREP

Look Ahead: Match selectively

You're working on a document with lots of graphs. The text contains many references to these graphs in the form of *Figure* followed by the relevant number. The publisher wants those references in bold – just the word *Figure*, not the number. It is easy to find these instances: just search for `Figure \d`. To apply the necessary formatting, specify bold in Change Format. But now you have a problem: the numbers appear in bold as well – this is not what we want. What we need to find is not *Figure* and a following number, but only the word *Figure* if it is followed by a number. This can be done with the following expression:

Find what: `Figure(?=\s\d)`
Change to: <leave empty>
Change format: Bold

Try this expression and check that InDesign selects instances of *Figure* only when it is followed by a digit, and that it does not select that digit. (It won't select the space between *Figure* and the digit either, as we included that space in the parenthetical.) Naturally, to cope with references such as *in Figures 5 and 6* we have to allow for *Figures*, which is easy: just add `s?`: `Figures?(?=\s\d)`.

The construct we used here is called "positive look-ahead", and can be selected from the Match flyout. Its general format is `(?= )`; after the `=` symbol any regular expression can be used. We'll see more examples soon.

In some cases, typically when you don't need to apply formatting, you can choose between lookaheads and other approaches. For example, to change *figure* to *Figure* when it is followed by a digit, you could use either of these methods:

Find what: `figure(?=\s\d)`
Change to: `Figure`
Find what: `figure(\s\d)`
Change to: `Figure$1`

The first method uses a lookahead; the second one captures the digit (and any preceding space), creating a reference, and uses that reference in the replace string (`$1`). In general, when you want to apply any formatting to some part of what you search, you'll have to use look-aheads. But even when you don't have to, I think you're better off using lookahead rather than replacement with a variable, because using lookahead is less disruptive and probably quicker as well.

Adjust space between certain characters

Any GREP expression can be used in the lookahead. Here is an example with a character class. In some typefaces, the *f* has a big overhang so that it collides with or is too close to the ascenders of some letters even when there's a space in between (as you can see earlier in this sentence,

68

where the f gets too close to the 'has'). Bembo and Gara-
mond are notable examples of such typefaces. To add a
bit of space after any *f* when followed by a space and *b*, *h*,
k, *l*, or *t*, place the space and a character class consisting
of these ascender letters in a lookahead and set some
tracking value in the Change Format area.

Find what: f(?=\s[bhkl])
Change to: <leave empty>
Change format: some tracking

You must use lookahead here: when you use the GREP
f\s[bhkl], tracking is applied to the space and the *b*, *h*, *k*, or
l as well, which is wrong.

Small caps revisited

For a slightly more complicated example, let us look again
at applying Small Caps to series of capitals. Earlier we
saw that this is easy to handle with these expressions:

Find what: \u\u+
Change to: <leave blank>
Change format: OpenType All Small Caps

This is fine. However, most publishers require some
spacing for small capitals. You could add this space when
you apply OT smallcaps style – in other words, add some
tracking at Change Format – but that is not strictly speaking correct, as that would add some space after the last
smallcapped letter as well. This means that OT smallcaps needs to be applied to all capitals, but tracking must
not be applied to the last. To achieve this, after applying
smallcaps as above, do this:

Find what: `\u+(?=\u)`
Change to: <leave blank>
Change format: Some tracking

This GREP expression finds series of capitals that are followed by one capital, but does not select the last capital because it's in a lookahead. (The method described here works for OT Pro fonts, but may not work for all fonts.) Here we have another example of a task that needs two passes to accomplish; to chain two or more expressions, see the section "Chaining GREP Queries" on page 61.

Negative lookahead

In the examples shown so far, we have selected things based on what follows – positive lookahead. There's also negative lookahead `(?! )`, which is positive lookahead's negative counterpart. It is entirely straightforward: it is used to match something only when it is *not* followed by what is specified in the lookahead. For instance, to find all instances of *Figure* and *Figures* not followed by a digit, use the following expression (the exclamation mark is used for negation):

`Figures?(?!\s\d)`

Lookbehind

In addition to looking ahead, you can also look back (or "behind", as it's called in the world of GREP). There are two formats for positive lookbehind: `(?<= )` and `\K`. The former, `(?<= )`, is the classic lookbehind generally available in GREP implementations, and was present when

70

GREP was added to InDesign in CS3. \K was introduced in CS6, is easier to use, and is more efficient, but for the sake of compatibility with pre-CS6 versions of InDesign we illustrate both formats here.

Italicise prefixed words

For example, to italicise all words with the prefix *over* but not that prefix itself, do this:

> Find what: (?<=over)\w+ or over\K\w
> Change to: <leave blank>
> Change format: Italics

Italicise letters following a year

For another example, we turn again to bibliographies. When an author has more than one publication in one year, these publications are distinguished by placing a letter after the year (2007a, 2007b, 2007c, etc.) Many publishers want these letters italicised. To find them, all we need to do is formulate a lookbehind to match four digits:

> Find what: (?<=\d\d\d\d)[a-z] or \d\d\d\d\K[a-z]
> Change to: <leave blank>
> Change format: Italics

We could have used \l (for "any lower-case letter") instead of [a-z] – it doesn't make any difference.

Use table figures after capitals

In a text that uses oldstyle figures by default, it is often better to use lining figures in combination with capitals, as in *C4* and *DK23*, which looks better than *C4* and

DK23. To find numbers preceded by a capital and apply lining-figure style, do this:

Find what: (?<=\u)\d+ or \u\K\d+
Change to: <leave blank>
Change format: Open Style features, one of the lining-figure styles.

A limitation of the classic lookbehind

Lookbehind has a limitation in that the expression that it contains must match items of the same length. In the last example we could use lookbehind to apply a lining-figure style to numbers following a capital. For example, if you want to apply lining-figure style when the capital and the number are separated by a hyphen, you'd be tempted to use (?<=\u-?)\d+. But that doesn't work. Instead, we need to list the alternatives:

Find what: ((?<=\u)|(?<=\u-))\d+

Broken down:

(start grouping
(?<=\u) lookbehind: upper case
| or
(?<=\u-) lookbehind: upper case followed by hyphen
) end grouping
\d+ one or more digits

Here the workaround is simple, but that's not always the case. In *Mastering Regular Expressions*, Friedl notes that all implementations of GREP have this limitation, so InDesign's GREP is no different in this regard. According to Friedl, variable-width lookbehind is too complex to handle. In any event, the upshot is that in classic lookbehind expressions you can't use any of the operators *, +, ?, or {n}. As we have seen, this limitation does not apply to lookahead.

The limitations noted here do not apply to the \K-type lookbehind. So you can use \u-?\K\d+ for the expression discussed above. Alternatives, too, become much easier to read. For example, to find numbers preceded by Figure, Map, or Table, and capture just the numbers, you can use (Figure|Map|Table)\s\K\d+.

Negative lookbehind

Like negative lookahead, there's negative lookbehind as well. It, too, is straightforward: it tells InDesign to match things that are not preceded by a certain string. The general format is (?<!); to find digits not preceded by *Chapter*, use: (?<!Chapter\s)\d

All rules applying to GREP expressions apply to what you use in lookaheads and lookbehinds. Escaping special GREP characters is one of those rules. To find all dollar prices, for instance – that is, to find any string preceded by a dollar symbol and made up of digits, commas, and dots – use (?<=\$)[\d.,]+. As the dollar symbol means "end of paragraph" in regular expressions, to find dollar symbols in a document you need to search for \$.

The newer positive lookbehind \K doesn't have a negative version.

Lookaround

Lookaheads and lookbehinds can be combined in what is called "lookaround". This isn't provided as a selection in InDesign's interface, reasonably, because you can simply select lookbehind and lookahead. Some examples follow.

Match words wrapped in certain characters

To italicise all words in a document that occur in double quotation marks but not the quotation marks themselves, use this query:

Find what: `(?<=")[-\w]+(?=")`
Change to: <select italics at Change Format>

Keep certain words together

In Polish typography, the single-letter prepositions *w* and *z* (both are general locative prepositions meaning "in", "at", and "by", and "from", "off", respectively) shouldn't be separated from the following noun or adjective. The neatest way to format them is to replace the space between the two words with a variable-width non-breaking space, which can be done as follows:

Find what: `(?i)(?<=\b[wz])\s(?=\w)`
Change to: `~S`

Broken down:

`(?i)` ignore case
`(?<=` start lookbehind
`\b[wz]` w or z at the beginning of a word
`)` stop lookbehind
`\s` any space

(?=\w) a word character

We use the case-insensitive modifier so that *W*, *w*, *Z*, and *z* are all found. The find expression matches spaces that are preceded by *w/W* or *z/Z* and followed by any word character. We need to specify the word boundary \b in the lookbehind, of course.

The expression given here for Polish can be useful in English, too, to satisfy the demands of publishers who don't want *I* (the first-person pronoun) and *a* (the indefinite article) dangling at the end of a line. In fact, for English it's a bit easier as we can match any single-letter word:

Find what: (?<=\b\w)\s(?=\w)
Change to: ~S

In English, *I* and *A/a* exhaust the class of single-letter words, so we needn't bother with a character class.

Replace hyphens in page ranges – revisited

To illustrate negative lookaround, we turn to a trickier example. Earlier we mentioned that we can't use the word boundary marker \b to distinguish between page ranges and longer series of hyphenated numbers (such as ISBN, telephone, and grant numbers). That's because the hyphen is considered a word boundary. Thus, the expression (?x) \b (\d+) - (\d+) \b (spaces added for clarity) matches numbers with any number of hyphens.

To match page ranges, we need to say something like "two numbers separated by a hyphen, the first number mustn't be preceded by a digit or a hyphen, and the second number mustn't be followed by a hyphen or a digit". This mouthful can be captured by the following GREP expression:

`(?<![-\d])(\d+)-(\d+)(?![-\d])`

Broken down:

      `(?<!` start negative lookbehind
    `[-\d]` hyphen or digit
       `)` end negative lookbehind
    `(\d+)` one or more digits
      `-` hyphen
    `(\d+)` one or more digits
     `(?!` start negative lookahead
    `[-\d]` hyphen or digit
      `)` end negative lookahead

We have to use the character class `[-\d]` to check for the presence of the word boundary – just checking for hyphens isn't enough. You can see that if you change the two instances of `[-\d]` to just -, we match *234-56* in *234-567-890*.

Lookaround and formatting

With lookbehind and lookahead you can match text when it is preceded or followed by certain text. This is limited to text only: you can say, "Find an f followed by a closing parenthesis" (using the expression `f(?=\))`), but you can't create an expression that says, "Find an italic f followed by a roman closing parenthesis". In other words, any formatting that you set in Find Format applies to the whole GREP expression.

However, with some GREP trickery it is possible to match text depending on the presence of formatting. It is easy to convert formatting codes to text tags (HTML-like tags, for instance). With such text tags you can then use lookaround to find roman text only when it is preceded or followed by a tag that represents italic text (or any other formatting, but we'll use italic here for illustration). When you're done, you convert from tags back to formatted text.

Changing formatting to text tags

This is much less complicated than it sounds, and a few examples will bear that out. For example, to mark all italic with the tags *<i>* and *</i>* use these expressions:

Find what: .+
Find format: +Italic
Change to: <i>$0</i>
Change format: +Regular

This adds *<i>* wherever a stretch of italic text begins and *</i>* wherever it ends. It also removes all italic from the text, which, as we'll see later, is necessary. Thus, a sentence such as "let's get rid of *all* italics codes" will appear as "let's get rid of <i>all</i> italic codes". Now that the tags have been inserted, you can use them in any GREP expression. For example, to find an italic f followed by roman closing parenthesis, use this:

Find what: f</i>\K\)

Broken down:

      f</i> f followed by </i>
        \K End of lookbehind

\) closing parenthesis

In other words, "match closing parentheses only if they're preceded by an f which itself followed by </i>".

Another useful application is to swap a character and a tag. Take a text that has run-in headers such as *Keywords:* and *Note:*. We want the colons roman, not italic, so we want to move the colon out of the italic font style; in other words, we want swap the italic-on tag and the colon. This isn't immediately possible in InDesign, but when we make the formatting visible it is simple. After converting the formatting to tags, our example words look like <i>Keywords:</i> and <i>Note:</i>. Because the colons should be roman with other possible italic words as well, all that is needed is to swap the character and the tag in this way:

Find what: :</i>
Change to: </i>:

Finally, an example to remove italic from quotes, as in *"Misplaced italic"*, which we want to change to *"Misplaced italic"*:

Find what: <i>"(.+?)"</i>
Change to: "<i>$1</i>"

Broken down:

<i>" match <i>"

(.+?) capture any characters, shortest match

"</i> up to "</i>

Changing text tags to formatting

When you're done manipulating the codes, you revert to proper italic formatting using these expressions:

Find what: <i>(.+?)</i>
Change to: $1
Change format: +Italic

Ideally, the set of GREP expressions that convert formatting to tags and the set that converts the tags back to formatting will be saved as queries. Call them, say, italic_1 and italic_2. Whenever you want to convert italics to tags, run italic_1; to revert to italic formatting, run italic_2.

Text tags such as these can be put to good use for several other things. One application is cleaning up imported documents. When you import a document and convert all formatting to tags, you can see all kinds of formatting irregularities that are barely visible otherwise. Italicised space characters, for instance, become visible as <i> </i>. Such tags can be deleted, and the superfluous formatting thus removed, by using these expressions:

Find what: <i>(\s)</i>
Change to: $1

We use \s here rather than the literal space so that we include returns, tabs, and all other forms of white space. Another type of ghost is visible in "let's get rid of the <i>italic</i> <i>codes</i>", where we see an unnecessary font change for the space between *italic* and *codes*. The expressions that handle such cases are almost identical to the previous one:

Find what: `</i>(\s)<i>`
Change to: `$1`

The examples given here involve italics, but any other formatting can be handled in a similar way: bold, semi-bold, underline, strikethrough, super- and subscript – any code at all. You need to store each set of expressions in separate queries, so you may end up with italic_1, under-line_1, bold_1, super_1, sub_1, etc., to convert formatting to tags, and italic_2, underline_2, and so on, to revert to InDesign formatting later. Naturally, running all these queries separately in InDesign requires is a nightmare, but you can chain GREP queries using the method described in "Chaining GREP Queries" on page 61.

Once you've created a number of queries to convert different types of formatting to text codes, the queries to clean up the tags can be generalised and their number thus reduced. The query is as follows:

Find what: `</(\w)>(\s)<\1>`
Change to: `$2`

Broken down:

`<`	match <
`/(\w)`	match / and capture a word character
`>`	match >
`(\s)`	capture white space
`<`	match <
`\1`	match what was captured in the first parenthetical
`>`	match >

If you're not sure that using single letters between angled brackets is safe enough for using this type of tag (they might be used for other purposes, which is sometimes the case in mathematical texts), you can use different symbols for the angle brackets, or you can use more elaborate codes, such as <italic> and </italic>. The expressions that generalise tags in the latter case need a tiny adjustment:

Find what: `</(\w+)>(\s)<\1>`
Change to: `$1`

We added just a plus sign after the first `\w` so that all word characters between angled brackets are captured.

13

Other Operations

Replacing using location markers

It is easy to insert text before or after a certain character. For example, to insert a tab after a bullet, simply replace each bullet with itself and a tab: find ~8, replace with ~8\t. This approach works both in the Text and the GREP tabs of the Find/Change dialog and is entirely straightforward.

But what if you want to insert text at the beginning or end of a word, paragraph, or story? We saw earlier that location markers match a position, not a character – so what does this mean when you replace things? After all, you can't replace the start of a story or a word. It seems obvious that these location markers cannot be replaced, but you can use them to find something and ignore them for the replacement. For example, to replace all numbers in a non-automatically numbered list with a bullet, you could use these expressions:

Find what: ^\d+\.?
Change to: ~8

The search expression paraphrases as "Find beginning of paragraph followed by one or more digits, perhaps followed by a dot". ^, the beginning-of-paragraph marker, is used for the search, but for the replacement it has no meaning. This replacement works because apart from the location marker there is some text that GREP can work with.

All this means that location markers can be used to insert something at a location, but since the location marker is not a character, you need some kind of character to get a handle on the position right before or after the location marker. Another example will make that clear. Suppose you want to insert a symbol, say a bullet, at the end of all stories in a document. You would need these expressions:

Find what: (.)\z
Change to: $1~8

Trying to replace \z, the end-of-story marker, with ~8\z won't work: you need a "real" character to get the replacement done, and in this case that's the character preceding the end-of-story marker – in other words, the last character in the story. As you want to add a character, you need to create a reference to that last character and put it back into the story; that's what (.) and the reference to it, $1, do. the query therefore paraphrases as "replace the last character in the story with itself and a bullet".

A slightly more complicated example is to add a period at the end of paragraphs when there isn't one. We need to take into account paragraphs which end with some other punctuation, such as exclamation and question marks. We therefore need to find paragraphs which do not end in a period, exclamation mark, or question mark and add a period. This query, which uses a negative character class, will handle that:

Find what: ([^.?!])$
Change to: $1.

If the last character in a paragraph is not one of the three punctuation marks, it is replaced by itself and a period is added. (Depending on the spelling conventions used in the text you're dealing with you might need to add parentheses and quotation marks to the the character class.)

A more complicated example inserts an em space before the source of a quote when that quote is a parenthetical at the end of that quote, in this common format:

> Avenirma se pessinatquo ves videt istissi movitiam nos, Patquam dum plicaed faute a vis, ve, non vivas interbentus, oraedium fin vid ia acturorum am inatodi cibutem iumust inatus, me forum ad rem morei praesest grae adhui iamdieris hilicit num ni pris. (Tam ina Sati, ves!) Serum num se convent ebatorbit. Tu que cestarteres! Scit patantes? Ahabeffremo culic vis parenium nocci poraequ itatim implientrum terferunt.|(Quasimodo, annis mirabilis)

In other words, we're after the last instance of *space+(* in the paragraph – it's highlighted in the example above – and we want to replace it with an em space. First we need to find the last parenthetical. When I tried, my first attempt was \(.+?\)$ – everything from (to the paragraph-ending), shortest match, .+?. This failed as it matched everything from the first (to the last), that is, from *(Tam ina* to *mirabilis)*. I hadn't expected that, but it does make sense: my GREP expression matches from the first (to the last) in the paragraph, and though I had specified "shortest match", that still included some opening and closing parentheses in between.

Another approach I tried was "match everything between (and the last) in a paragraph *without intervening)*", which is expressed as \([^)]+\)$. This worked fine; it breaks down as follows:

\(match an opening parenthesis

[^)]+ continue matching while not a closing parenthesis

\) then match that parenthesis . . .

$ . . . at the end of the paragraph.

But this matches the whole parenthetical, which is not correct: we need to match just the space preceding it, so we need to cast the GREP expression as a lookahead following a space. This is the complete query:

Find what: \s(?=\([^)]+\)$)
Change to: ~m

Single-line and multiline

In the Modifiers flyout are two sets of modifiers, Single-line On/Off and Multiline On/Off. These modifiers influence the behaviour of the . wildcard ("match everything") and the location markers ^ (beginning of paragraph) and $ (paragraph end).

Single-line mode determines the behaviour of . (the dot wildcard). When single-line mode is off, which is GREP's default state, .* matches everything from the cursor position to the end of the paragraph, except the para-graph mark itself. Use (?s) to enable single-line mode and .* ignores paragraph marks, selecting everything from the insertion point to the end of the story. If there is no insertion point and you have a text frame selected, (?s).* selects the whole story – not just the text in the selected text frame – including any overset text.

The single-line/multiline settings influence the behaviour of ^ and $. When multiline is enabled, which is the default state, ^ and $ match the beginning and the end of each paragraph, respectively; they respect para-graph boundaries. If multiline is disabled with (?-m), ^ and $ ignore the paragraph boundaries and become in effect beginning-of-story and end-of-story markers – synony-mous with \A and \z.

Conditional GREP expressions

The techniques demonstrated up to now in this guide are all frequently applied. In this section we show a rather less common construct, and though you'll probably need it less often than the expression types discussed earlier (if at all), it can be useful to have this advanced method in your arsenal. We'll give a few examples.

Suppose you want to match a word, say *quick*, and, if it occurs in square brackets, those brackets as well. You define this strictly: either two brackets or none. So you want *quick* and *[quick]*, but not *[quick* or *quick]*. Some experiments show that including the brackets as optional, \[?quick\]?, isn't any good because it would give you *quick* with just the opening or the closing bracket as well.

So we're looking for something like "match the closing bracket only when there is a match for the opening
bracket" – in other words, a match is made conditional on
an earlier match. You can write this as a GREP expression
as follows (the conditional is underlined):

`(?x)   (\[)?   quick   (?(1)\])`

What happens is this: with `(\[)?` we try to match an
opening square bracket; the question mark indicates that
the expression may or may not match. Then it matches
quick. Then follows the conditional: `(?(1)\])` paraphrases
as "if there was a match for the first capturing parenthesis, referred to here by `(1)` – in other words, if *quick*
is preceded by a bracket – then match a closing bracket
now". If there was no match before *quick*, a match won't
be attempted after it. The general format of the if–then
conditional, therefore, is `(?(condition)match)`. A more intel-
ligible expression that amounts to the same is this:

`(?x)   (\[quick\])   |   (?<\[)quick(?!\])`

which paraphrases as "quick preceded by [and] or quick
not preceded by [and]".

If–then–else constructions are possible, too, and have
the format `(?(condition)match|othermatch)`. This looks
daunting but an example will make it clear. Dutch infini-
tives end in *en*; *werken* means "to work" and *vullen* is "to
fill", for instance. Most Dutch past participles begin with
ge and end in *t* or *d*. The past participle of *werken* is *ge-
werkt* "(has) worked", that of *vullen* is *gevuld*. To find both
the infinitive and the past-participle form of a verb, we
need to find words that end in *en* and words that begin

87

with *ge* and end in *t* or *d*. Loosely formulated: "if you can match *ge* at the beginning of a word, then match *t* or *d* at the end; else (i.e. if there's no match for initial *ge*), match *en* at the end of a word. The expression is as follows:

```
(?x)  (ge)?   \w+   (?(1)[dt]|en)
```

This catches regular simple verb forms. The reality can be a bit more complicated but this is a decent start, and we'll leave it at that.

GREP Styles

GREP styles are a powerful tool to format text automatically (to see just how powerful, see Laurent Tournier's trick at *http://tinyurl.com/yes63gs*.) They are one of the three types of nested style – the other two are Nested Styles and Nested Line Styles.

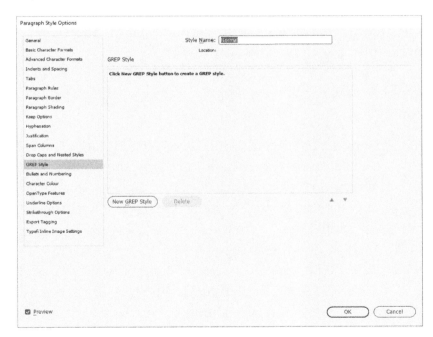

FIGURE 9. GREP styles

GREP styles are in fact normal character styles that are applied by GREP expressions defined in the Paragraph panel or the Paragraph Style Options dialog. Note that this involves only applying styles: you won't be able to change any text using GREP styles. In addition, you can't include formatting in the match, so it's not possible, say, to match certain strings in italics, at least not without converting to tags as described in "Lookaround and formatting" on page 76. Nevertheless, GREP styles are a powerful tool. As they are best defined in paragraph styles, that's what we'll illustrate here, but it works the same in the Paragraph panel.

To illustrate how to use GREP styles, we'll implement into them a few of our earlier examples. Some more elaborate examples follow this general outline.

Let's begin with a GREP style that, once defined, applies small caps to any sequence of more than one capital.

1. Define a character style as usual, call it "smallcaps", and set "OpenType All Small Caps" as part of its definition (in the Character Style Options dialog, go to Basic Character Formats, then pick "OpenType All Small Caps" from the Case dropdown).
2. Now go into the Paragraph Style Options dialog. Edit the paragraph style to which you want to add the GREP style by picking GREP Styles from the list on the left-hand side of the dialog.

3. In the GREP Style panel, click New GREP Style. A skeleton entry is created consisting of two items (see **FIGURE 9**).

4. At Apply Style (where it says [None]) you specify the character style which should be applied by the GREP expression at To Text. Click on [None] or anywhere to its right to display a list of available character styles and select the style you want, in this case "smallcaps".

5. Now click To Text and enter the GREP expression that should match whatever you want to apply small caps to. We use the expression **\u\u+** here: a capital followed by at least one more capital (see **FIGURE 10**). (The **@,** widget to the right of the entry field opens the same flyout as the one in the Find/Change dialog shown earlier in **FIGURE 2**.)

6. Complete the style definition by clicking OK or pressing Return.

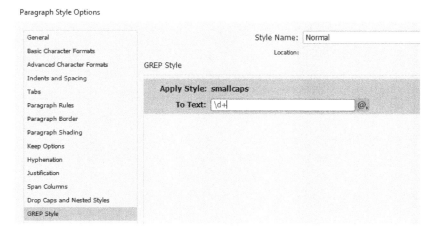

FIGURE 10. Add a GREP style

Let's check that our GREP style works. Draw a new text frame, select the paragraph style you just defined, and start typing. As soon as you type two or more consecutive capitals, the style is applied automatically. Magic!

You can define numerous other GREP styles, all in the same paragraph. Like all other paragraph features, GREP styles are inherited by a paragraph style's offspring (i.e. when you create a new paragraph style based on one with GREP styles), so you can have document-wide GREP styles by including them in a paragraph style on which all others are based. In this respect, GREP styles behave like all other formatting set in a paragraph style. It also means you need to be careful, because GREP styles have some performance impact on the document's handling. The more local you define GREP styles – that is, independent of styles based on it – the better.

Ordering GREP styles

As you probably know, when you apply a character style to some text in a document, any character style already applied to that text will be cancelled. Thus, if you have some text in which italics is applied by a character style and you then apply superscript to part of that text range again using a character style, the result is just superscript: the application of the superscript character style wipes out the italics.

GREP styles work better: you can apply several character styles using GREP styles and their formatting supplement each other. Thus if, using GREP styles, you apply italics and superscript to the same text range, the result is superscripted italics.

However, when two GREP styles apply different formatting of the same type, then the style that was applied last wins out. For instance, if you apply italics using a GREP style, and then apply bold using another GREP style, then that text range will be bold. Thus, the order of GREP styles in the dialog can be important.

Apply fonts to Unicode ranges

This is a set of GREP styles I set in almost all documents. The idea is to apply certain fonts to certain Unicode ranges. Ranges I use a lot are phonetics and mathematics. Some of my favourites are styles that apply a font to some Unicode ranges: a character style with a phonetic font is applied to `[\x{0250}-\x{02FF}]+` and another character style with a symbol font is applied to math operators, arrows, etc.: `[\x{2190}-\x{2BFF}]+`.

Applying styles in a table of contents

Tables of contents are good candidates for styling with GREP styles: their structure is consistent and they often need several styles applied to them.

Take the following two paragraphs. They are entries in a table of contents of a journal. The first entry refers to an article: author in bold, affiliation in italics and in parentheses, followed by a colon. The title in roman type, followed by an em space and the page number in a different typeface.

Justin Glover & T. A. Hall (*Bloomington*): The historical development of [ɡ] and [b] in a regional German dialect   **219**

Bjarke Frellesvig & John Whitman eds.: Proto-Japanese. (Series IV, Current Issues in Linguistic Theory, Volume 294). Reviewed by **Yoshizo Itabashiy** (*Kyushu*)   **401**

The second entry is from the review section in the same table of contents. It is similar to the first item. The author's affiliation is again in parentheses and in italics after the author's name in bold, but the review author's name is now at the end of the entry preceding the page number reference.

The formatting in both types of entry can be applied by one set of GREP styles. The first step is to create character styles for bold, italics, and the typeface for the page number reference at the end of the entry; in what follows we assume the presence of these styles. The GREP expressions used to format the example paragraphs are illustrated in **FIGURE 11**.

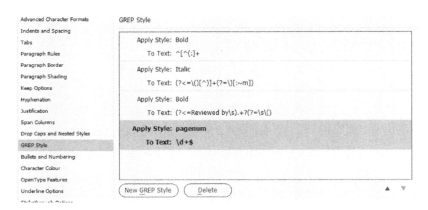

FIGURE 11. Formatting text with GREP styles

Some comments clarify the expressions:

Author name: `^[^(:]+`

Broken down:

`^` beginning of paragraph

`[^(:]+` up to the first (or :

The first style to be applied is bold to the name of the author of an article or the author of the reviewed book. This is always from the beginning of the paragraph (`^`) up to but not including the first parenthesis or colon (`[^(:]+`). (We could also have used `^.+?(?=[(:])`, which has the same effect.)

Affiliation: `(?<=\()[^)]+(?=\)[:~m])`

Broken down:

`(?<=\()` start after the first (

`[^)]+` up to the next)

`(?=\)` followed by a) . . .

`[:~m])` . . . and a colon or an em space.

The second style we apply is italics to the author's affiliation. In the case of an article, that's the first paren- thetical followed by a colon; and in the case of a review, the last parenthetical followed by an em space (`~m`; the em space is already present, it was placed there when the table of contents was generated.) The parentheses are placed in a lookbehind (`(?<=\()` and a lookahead (`(?=\)[:~m])` because they should not be styled.

Review author: `(?<=Reviewed by\s).+?(?=\s\()`

Broken down:

(?<=	begin lookbehind
Reviewed by\s	literal text
)	end lookbehind
.+?	one or more characters
(?=	begin lookahead
\s\(	a space and a (
)	end lookahead

The author of a review is easy to find: it is the text between *Reviewed by:* and the next opening parenthesis. Naturally, both these must be in a lookbehind and a lookahead to ensure that bold is applied to the autor's name only.

Finally, the page number is easy:

Page number: \d+$

The page number is matched by all digits (\d+) at the end of the paragraph ($).

How to optimise GREP expressions

It doesn't always matter whether a GREP expression is efficient, because GREP searches and replacements are very quick. But because GREP expressions in GREP styles execute every time a paragraph changes, long documents with many GREP styles tend to get sluggish and it therefore pays to optimise the expressions. Here are some tips:

Avoid * whenever you can: Use + instead

The difference between + and * is small (match one or more vs. match zero or more), but if you use * when you could have used +, you make InDesign work harder than necessary. For example, if you're looking for strings of upper-case letters, then \u* finds not only upper-case letters, but every insertion point in the document: \u* stands for "zero or more upper-case letters", and zero upper-case letters can be found at every insertion point! \u+ is far more efficient.

When you look for series of characters, start with two

When you want to replace, say, strings of spaces with a single space, look for \x20\x20+. When you look for \x20+, you replace every space, including single ones with a single space. Very inefficient. (I use \x20 here for clarity, you can type a space character.)

Use [^]+ instead of .+? wherever possible

To find text between, say, quotation marks, you can use ".+?" or "[^"]+". The former is easier to read, but the latter is quicker, though it can't always be used. See "Shortest match or negative character class?" on page 33 for details.

Use location whenever possible

The more explicit your GREP expression, the quicker it executes. If what you're after is always at the beginning of a paragraph, use ^ to tell InDesign not to look anywhere else but the beginning of the paragraph.

Don't use single-character alternatives: Use a character class

Character classes are more efficient than single-character alternatives. Thus, gr(a|e)y and gr[ae]y are functionally equivalent, but the second version, the character class, is more efficient.

Don't use ( ) if you don't have to

Parentheses create references, which takes time. If there's no real need to use parentheses, then don't. In the GREP expression (a|e), the parentheses are not necessary: a|b does the same job, but more efficiently. If you do have to use parentheses, use non-capturing groups; see the next point.

Use non-capturing groups

Sometimes parentheses have to be used to create a group of certain letters or words. If you don't need a reference to such a group, use a so-called non-capturing group. For instance, in a (blue|green) shirt the parentheses are needed because without them the expression would match just "a blue" and/or "green shirt". If you don't need any reference to green or blue, use a (?:blue|green) shirt expression instead. ?: tells InDesign not to create a reference for the text or the pattern in the parentheses.

When to optimise

Some of these optimising techniques don't do much for readability, especially negative character classes and non-capturing groups. To make life a little easier, you could use them only in places where they matter, which is typically in GREP styles.

Temporarily disabling GREP styles

You can disable one or more GREP styles temporarily by adding an asterisk at the beginning of the GREP expressions. For example, the second GREP style in **FIGURE 12** doesn't do anything at all. To reenable it, just remove the asterisk. This trick simply makes the GREP expression unwellformed so that it doesn't match anything.

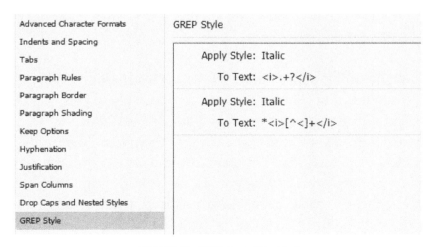

FIGURE 12. GREP Style Disabled

99

GREP styles, nested styles, and nested line styles

As mentioned earlier, GREP styles are in fact a type of nested style, even though they're in a separate section in the Paragraph Style Options dialog. It is clear that there is some opportunity for conflict – after all, each of these three types of style may want to format the same piece of text. When line, nested, and GREP styles apply different types of formatting to the same text there is no conflict and all are applied – in other words, they're complementary. But when they apply different instances of the same formatting (different type sizes, different fonts, etc.), we do have a conflict. This is solved by the order in which the styles are applied: line styles first, then nested styles, and GREP styles last. This means that whenever there is a conflict, GREP styles overrule any of the other two types of style, and nested styles overrule line styles. It is not possible to change the order in which line, nested, and GREP styles apply.

Copying GREP expressions from queries to GREP styles

When defining GREP styles, it's not possible to pick expressions directly from saved queries. To avoid re-keying expressions you can copy them from the Find/Change dialog and paste them into the GREP Style section, but be careful when you do this: some characters don't like the trip. For instance, \t and \r arrive as an open square (the literals of these codes can't be displayed in the dialog and are shown as squares), \s as a space. That \t is replaced with a square is of no consequence: the GREP will work fine. The literal for \r on the other hand disables the GREP entirely. Finally, that \s is replaced with a space changes the meaning of the GREP: \s stands for any white space, the space character for just the space character. Beware.

These problems can be avoided by using a script posted at *www.kahrel.plus.com/indesign/grep_query_manager. html.* The script displays an overview of all your GREP queries, allowing you to select any of these queries and copy the Find What string to any paragraph styles you select. So you can copy not only a single GREP expression to a single paragraph style, but also groups of expressions to groups of paragraph styles.

15

Troubleshooting

GREP is a symbolic system, and it is easy to lose track of certain formal aspects. We're not helped by GREP's interface: entering complex expressions can be a challenge in such a confined space, and the miniscule type in the Find What and Change to fields doesn't help either. Nor are we warned about errors in an expression: InDesign accepts anything. Recalcitrant expressions can be frustrating, but there are a number of things to look out for when troubleshooting expressions.

Patch to InDesign's latest version
Always try to use the latest version of InDesign. Check the CC app, it will tell you if there's an updated version.

Escape characters
It is easy to forget to escape certain characters, so if an expression doesn't work this is the first thing to check. Characters to be escaped are the ones that have a special meaning for GREP: . $? ^ * ( ) [ ] { } + |. For example, if you're looking for a digit in parentheses, be sure to escape the parentheses: \(\d\).

Some of these characters are problematic. For instance, various versions of InDesign have difficulty matching the dollar symbol ($). This is awkward because you can't find dollar prices: \$[\d.,]+ doesn't work as expected. The workaround in many cases is to use the character's Unicode value: \x{0024}[\d.,]+ does match dollar prices. Another possibility is to use the dollar symbol as a character class: [$][\d.,]+.

GREP is case-sensitive

Remember that GREP is case-sensitive by default, which is easy forget since text-based find-and-replace features are typically case-insensitive by default.

Hyphens in character classes

In character classes, when using a hyphen, always put it first or last. In [a-e], the hyphen is interpreted as a range symbol; the expression matches a, b, c, d, and e. In [-ae] it is seen as hyphen, and this expression matches -, a, and e.

The dot does not match footnote markers

The expression .+ should match whole paragraphs because the dot wildcard matches everything except the paragraph marker. But an InDesign bug causes . not to match the footnote marker so that if a paragraph contains a footnote, .+ matches only to the footnote. The workaround is to use .+(~F.+)?. (Endnote markers are no problem.)

Parentheses

Parentheses are used often in GREP, and it's necessary to ensure that each opening or closing parenthesis has a matching one on the other side.

Split complex expressions

Partly because of the limitations of its interface, it is useful to split complex expressions into smaller ones (see "Splitting Up Complex GREP Expressions" on page 53). That way they're easier to understand and modify, and far easier to correct when something goes wrong. If running separate expressions becomes tiresome, consider the script described in "Chaining GREP Queries" on page 61.

Spaces

Perhaps you typed a space somewhere. Spaces in GREP expressions must match spaces in your document, so they could cause the expression not to find anything. Use the `(?x)` modifier at the start of an expression if you want to use spaces for clarity.

You're trying a GREP search using the text search tab

Accidentally hitting the Page Up key moves the focus from the GREP tab to the Text search tab, and before you know it you're typing a GREP expression in the wrong Find What field. Press the Page Down key (or press Command/Ctrl+2) to move the focus back to the GREP tab.

Try GREP expressions on a small sample

We mentioned that InDesign accepts any GREP: it doesn't check syntax errors such as unbalanced parentheses. When your GREP doesn't find anything and you think it should, create a new document and add a small text frame with some text which your GREP should find something in. If it does find that text, at least you know that your GREP is in order.

Character-class mismatches

Make sure that character classes match characters in your documents the way you expect them to. In some cases there are mismatches. For example, in some of the Swiss and French versions of InDesign, \s doesn't match the same characters as in the English version. To see which characters are matched by certain character classes, use the system available at *www.kahrel.plus.com/indesign/ grep_mapper.html*.

16

Resources

InDesign's GREP uses the Boost libraries; information on these libraries is available from *www.boost.org*, especially *www.boost.org/doc/libs/1_67_0/libs/regex/doc/html/boost_regex/syntax/perl_syntax.html*.

The best resource for regular expressions is Jeffrey E.F. Friedl's *Mastering Regular Expressions* (O'Reilly). This title has a wealth of examples with detailed technical discussion about performance issues, and Friedl also provides interesting background and historical notes. Despite the high level of technicality here and there, the book is very readable, especially the first few introductory chapters. Virtually all the undocumented features I describe in this guide are due to Friedl's work: I simply tried several things he mentions to see if they worked in InDesign (and they usually did).

A tool to check which characters are matched by which character class is available at *www.kahrel.plus.com/indesign/grep_mapper.html*. Some more GREP tools are at *www.kahrel.plus.com/indesign/grep_matters.html*.

A more general kind of GREP tester can be found at *www.rorohiko.com/greptutor/GrepTutor.html*. This nice teaching tool lets you test any GREP expression.

A useful GREP analyser is Jongware's WhatTheGrep (*www.jongware.com/idgrephelp.html*). This tool deconstructs GREP expressions and applies colour codes to different elements of an expression, thus making them much more readable.

Gregor Fellenz's *InDesign automatisieren* (in German) contains an excellent chapter on GREP.

An interesting application of GREP styles can be found at *indesignsecrets.com/adventures-in-grepland.php*. Some of the best GREP-style trickery I've seen is in Laurent Tournier's *GREP et InDesign CS3/CS4. Rechercher, remplacer et formater en un clic* (Paris, Dunot). Laurent used to run a blog devoted exclusively to GREP in InDesign at *www.indigrep.com*. His blog has been quiet for a while but the posts are still available.

InDesign Magazine (*https://indesignsecrets.com/issues*) used to feature a useful column, GREP of the Month. Look through the back catalog to find them.

Various links relating to GREP matters can be found at *indesignsecrets.com/grep*.

17

Quick Reference

Character representations	
\x{nn}	Two-digit hexadecimal code. \x{20} represents the space character
\x{nnnn}	Four-digit hexadecimal code (Unicode): \x{0020} represents the space character
\N{unicode name}	Unicode names. \N{Latin small letter a with ogonek} represents ą. The Unicode's name is case-insensitive, but it matches case-sensitively. Thus, both \N{latin small letter a with ogonek} and \N{Latin Small letter A with ogonek} match ą

Character classes 1: Standard classes

I call these classes "standard" for lack of a better term. They were part of the first implementations of GREP, and of the three types of class, to this day the standard classes are the easiest to use.

Standard classes	
[char]	A single character or a group of characters
[^char]	Exclude single character or a group of characters
.	Any character except paragraph break
\w	Word character: letters, digits, and underscore
\W	Non-word character
\l	Lowercase letter
\L	Non-lower-case letter
\u	Uppercase letter
\U	Non-upper-case letter
\d	Digit
\D	Nondigit
\h	Horizontal space: all spaces and tabs
\H	Non-horizontal space characters
\s	Whitespace character: all spaces, tabs, and returns
\S	Non-whitespace character
\v	Vertical space: break characters – paragraph break, forced line break, page, column, frame breaks.
\V	Whatever is not \v

Character classes 2: Posix expressions

There is much overlap of the Posix class and the standard class. Most Posix expressions listed here can be easily formulated in terms of the standard classes, as indicated in the table below. Punctuation, too, could in principle be given using literals, but that would be awkward (and Unicode properties provide much more versatile search patterns; see next section). The list here omits some that will never be used in InDesign, such as [[:ctrl:]], which matches control characters. From CS4, Posix has become pretty much redundant: what I considered the only really useful Posix, the punctuation one, can now be replaced with its equivalent in the more versatile Unicode properties, illustrated in the next section.

Posix expressions	
[[:alnum:]]	Alphanumeric characters: letters and digits [\u\l\d]
[[:alpha:]]	Alphabetic characters [\u\l]
[[:digit:]]	Digits [\d]
[[:word:]]	Alphanumeric characters and the under-score character \w
[[:blank:]]	Spaces and tabs [\x20\t]
[[:graph:]]	Non-blank characters [^\x20\t]
[[:lower:]]	Lowercase letters \l
[[:upper:]]	Uppercase letters \u

Posix expressions *(continued)*	
[[:punct:]]	Punctuation
[[:space:]]	All whitespace characters \s
[[:xdigit:]]	Hexadecimal digits [0-9A-Fa-f]
[[.xy.]]	Digraphs entered as two separate letters. The recognised digraphs are *ae, Ae, AE, ch, Ch, CH, ll, Ll, LL, ss, Ss, SS, nj, Nj, NJ, dz, Dz, DZ, lj, Lj, LJ* (*oe, Oe*, and *OE* aren't matched)
[[.n.]]	Equivalent to \N{n}; see above

Character classes 3: Unicode properties

There's again much overlap between this class and the other two, but its refinements, such as distinguishing opening and closing punctuation, are often useful. They will be appreciated by people who work with Southeast Asian languages, as the Unicode properties recognise the scripts used by these languages.

There are seven basic Unicode properties (\p{L*}, \p{M*}, \p{Z*}, \p{S*}, \p{N*}, \p{P*}, and \p{C*}, each of which has a number of subproperties. The basic properties are in shaded cells in the table.

Unicode properties are flexible in their spelling, having short and long forms. The short forms are in the first column; the long forms introduce the explanation. Both forms are case- and space-insensitive: \p{lu}, \p{LU}, and \p{Lu} are equivalent, as are \p{lowercase_letter}, \p{low-ercaseletter}, \p{Lowercase_Letter}, \p{lowercase letter}, and whichever variant you can think of. Finally, using \P matches the negation of \p classes: \P{Lu}, for instance, matches anything that's not a capital.

Unicode Properties	
\p{L*}	\p{letter} Any letter; it's the combination of the following three classes.
\p{Ll}	\p{lowercase_letter}
\p{Lu}	\p{uppercase_letter}
\p{Lt}	\p{titlecase_letter} In some languages, digraphs have a special title-case form. InDesign matches *Dz* (Unicode 01F2), *Dž* (01C5), *Lj* (01C8), and *Nj* (01CB). Of the three forms of this type of letter, *nj* is matched by \p{Ll}, *NJ* by \p{Lu}, and *Nj* by \p{Lt}. Note that this works only if the digraphs are entered by their Unicode values.
	\p{titlecase_letter} matches the Ancient Greek letters with subscript iota as well, as they can be written with the subscript as a sepa-rate letter: Aι, Hι, Ωι, and their variants with diacritics.
\p{Lm}	\p{modifier_letter} Various spacing-modifier characters (Unicode 02B0–02FF).
\p{Lo}	\p{letter_other} Additional letters not captured by the four \p{L.} classes outlined above, i.e. letters without case and that aren't modi-fiers: characters from Hebrew, Arabic, the Southeast-Asian languages, etc.

Unicode Properties (continued)	
\p{M*}	\p{mark} Any of the following three types of mark.
\p{Mn}	\p{non_spacing_mark} Includes combining diacritical marks and tone marks. Matches characters in a wide variety of Unicode ranges.
\p{Mc}	\p{spacing_combining_mark} Vowels in South-east-Asian languages.
\p{Me}	\p{enclosing_mark} Circles, squares, keycaps, etc. Found in a variety of Unicode ranges.
\p{Z*}	\p{separator} Spaces, returns, line-separator character (2028), paragraph-separator character (2029). Doesn't include hyphens or dashes.
\p{Zs}	\p{space_separator} All spaces except tab and return.
\p{Zl}	\p{line_separator} Line-separator character (2028).
\p{Zp}	\p{paragraph_separator} Paragraph-separator character (2029).
\p{S*}	\p{symbol} Matches the following four classes.
\p{Sm}	\p{math_symbol} Math symbols.
\p{Sc}	\p{currency_symbol} All currency symbols.
\p{Sk}	\p{modifier_symbol} Combining characters with their own width, such as the acute accent 00B4 (not the acute accent from the Combining Dia-critical Marks range, 0301).

Unicode Properties *(continued)*

\p{So}	\p{other_symbol} Wingdings, dingbats, etc., from various ranges.
\p{N*}	\p{number} Any kind of number.
\p{Nd}	\p{decimal_digit_number} The digits 0 to 9.
\p{Nl}	\p{letter_number} The Roman upper- and lower-case numerals in Number forms (2150–218F).
\p{No}	\p{other_number} Superscripts and subscripts, fractions, enclosed numbers in Latin 1, number forms, and enclosed alphanumerics.
\p{P*}	\p{punctuation} Any of the following seven classes of punctuation mark.
\p{Pd}	\p{dash_punctuation} All hyphens and dashes.
\p{Ps}	\p{open_punctuation} Opening brackets, braces, parentheses, etc. (e.g. 2045, FE17, FF62).
\p{Pe}	\p{close_punctuation} Closing brackets, braces, parentheses, etc. (e.g. 2046, FE18, FF63).
\p{Pi}	\p{initial_punctuation} All opening quotes.
\p{Pf}	\p{final_punctuation} All closing quotes.
\p{Pc}	\p{connector_punctuation} underscore, ‿ (203F), ⁀ (2040), ⁀ (2054).
\p{Po}	\p{other_punctuation} All other punctuation: ! " % &, etc.
\p{C*}	\p{other} Appears to find just tabs and returns.

Unicode Properties (continued)

\p{Cc}	\p{control} Control characters in C0 Controls and Basic Latin (0000–0020), such as Tab and Esc.
\p{Cf}	\p{format} Various nonvisible formatting characters in General Punctuation (2000–206F): left-to-right and right-to-left markers, embedding, etc.
\p{Co}	\p{private_use} Characters in ranges not used by Unicode, intended for use by font developers (E000–F8FF).
\p{Cn}	\p{unassigned} Several unassigned unicode ranges (e.g. D7A4–D7FF).

Location Markers

^	Beginning of paragraph
$	End of paragraph
\b	Word boundary
\B	Not word boundary
\<	Beginning of word
\>	End of word
\A	Beginning of story
\Z or \z	End of story

Location markers (*continued*)	
(?=)	Positive lookahead
(?!)	Negative lookahead
(?<=)	Positive lookbehind
(?<!)	Negative lookbehind
( )	Group a pattern and capture matches into \1, \2 and $1, $2
\n	In an expression, contains the text matched by the nth capture group
$n	In a replacement string, contains the text matched by the nth capture group
(?:)	Group a subpattern, but don't capture match
x|y	Alternatives
*	Match 0 times or more
+	Match 1 time or more
?	Match 0 or 1 times
{x}	Match exactly x times
{x,}	Match at least x times
{x,y}	Match at least x times but not more than y times
*?	Match 0 or 1 times, but as few as possible (shortest match)
+?	Match 1 time or more, but as few as possible
??	Match 0 or 1 times, but as few as possible

Location markers (continued)

{x,}?	Match at least x times, but as few as possible
{x,y}?	Match at least x times but not more than y times, and as few as possible

Modifiers

(?i)	Case-insensitive match
(?-i)	Case-sensitive match (default)
(?#)	Comment
(?x)	Free-spacing mode (spaces in expressions are ignored)
(?m)	Multiline mode (^ and $ match at paragraph beginning and end; default)
(?-m)	Multiline mode off (^ and $ match at beginning and end of story)
(?s)	Single-line mode (the dot . matches up to the next paragraph ending; default)
(?-s)	Single-line mode off (the dot . matches up to the end of the story)
\Q ...\E	Literal-text span: GREP sees all characters literally, with * interpreted as an asterisk character rather than as a wildcard, [and] are taken as brackets rather than as defining a character class, etc.

GREP code dictionary

The list presents all codes, characters, and markers that can be used in GREP expressions. It is sorted by code so that unfamiliar GREP codes can be looked up easily.

Code	Description	Code	Description
\1	back-reference (up to \9)	\x{. . .}	two- or four-digit hexadecimal code
\A	beginning of story	\z	end of story
\b	word boundary	\Z	end of story
\d	digit	\\	backslash character
\D	non-digit	\[	open bracket character
\h	horizontal space	\]	close bracket character
\H	not horizontal space	\{	open brace character
\K	lookbehind	\}	close brace character
\l	(lowercase L) lower-case letter	\(	open parenthesis character
\L	non-lower-case letter	\)	close parenthesis character
\n	forced line break	\<	beginning of word
\N{. . .}	Unicode name	\>	end of word
\P{. . .}	negated unicode class	~2	copyright symbol
\p{. . .}	unicode class	~3	third space
\r	end of paragraph	~4	quarter space
\S	non-whitespace character	~6	section symbol
\s	whitespace character	~7	paragraph symbol
\t	tab character	~8	bullet character
\U	non-upper-case letter	~a	anchored-object marker
\u	upper-case letter	~b	carriage return (=\r)
\v	vertical space	~d	trademark symbol
\V	not vertical space	~D	variable: output date
\W	non-word character	~e	ellipsis
\w	word character		

~E even-page break
~f flush space
~F footnote marker
~h end nested style here
~H variable: chapter number
~i indent to here
~I (capital I) index marker
~j non-joiner
~J variable: metadata
    caption
~k discretionary line break
~L odd-page break
~l (lowercase L) variable: file
    name
~M column break
~m em-space
~N current page number
~O variable: creation date
~o variable: modifiation date
~P page break
~R frame break
~r registered symbol
~S non-breaking
~s non-breaking (fixed
    space)
~T variable: last page number
~u variable: custom text
~v any variable
~V previous page number
~X next page number

~x section marker
~y right-indent tab
~Y variable: running header
    (paragraph style)
~Z variable: running header
    (character style)
~# any page number
~" straight double quotation
    mark
~' straight single quotation
    mark
~- discretionary hyphen
~~ non-breaking hyphen
~. punctuation space
~/ figure space
~% sixth space
~| hair space
~[straight left quotation
    mark
~] straight right quotation
    mark
~{ double left quotation
    mark
~} double right quotation
    mark
~< thin space
~> en-space
~_ em-dash
~= en-dash

Printed in Great Britain
by Amazon